LYNDON B. JOHNSON

LYNDON B. JOHNSON

Tony Kaye

CHELSEA HOUSE PUBLISHERS
NEW YORK
PHILADELPHIA

EDITOR-IN-CHIEF: Nancy Toff
EXECUTIVE EDITOR: Remmel T. Nunn
MANAGING EDITOR: Karyn Gullen Browne
COPY CHIEF: Juliann Barbato
PICTURE EDITOR: Adrian G. Allen
ART DIRECTOR: Giannella Garrett
MANUFACTURING MANAGER: Gerald Levine

Staff for LYNDON B. JOHNSON:

SENIOR EDITOR: John W. Selfridge
ASSISTANT EDITORS: Sean Dolan, Kathleen McDermott
COPY EDITOR: Michael Goodman
ASSOCIATE PICTURE EDITOR: Juliette Dickstein
PICTURE RESEARCHER: Toby Greenberg
SENIOR DESIGNER: David Murray
ASSISTANT DESIGNER: Jill Goldreyer
PRODUCTION COORDINATOR: Joseph Romano
COVER ILLUSTRATION: David Dircks

CREATIVE DIRECTOR: Harold Steinberg

3 5 7 9 8 6 4

Library of Congress Cataloging in Publication Data

Kaye, Tony. LYNDON B. JOHNSON

(World leaders past & present)
Bibliography: p.
1. Johnson, Lyndon B. (Lyndon Baines), 1908–1973—
Juvenile literature. 2. Presidents—United States—
Biography—Juvenile literature. 3. United States—Politics
and government—1963–1969—Juvenile literature.
  I. Title. II. Series: World leaders past & present.
E847.K38   1988   973.923′092′4 [B]   87-20827

ISBN 0-87754-536-7
   0-7910-0579-8 (pbk.)

Contents

John Adams
John Quincy Adams
Konrad Adenauer
Alexander the Great
Salvador Allende
Marc Antony
Corazon Aquino
Yasir Arafat
King Arthur
Hafez al-Assad
Kemal Atatürk
Attila
Clement Attlee
Augustus Caesar
Menachem Begin
David Ben-Gurion
Otto von Bismarck
Léon Blum
Simon Bolívar
Cesare Borgia
Willy Brandt
Leonid Brezhnev
Julius Caesar
John Calvin
Jimmy Carter
Fidel Castro
Catherine the Great
Charlemagne
Chiang Kai-Shek
Winston Churchill
Georges Clemenceau
Cleopatra
Constantine the Great
Hernán Cortés
Oliver Cromwell
Georges-Jacques
  Danton
Jefferson Davis
Moshe Dayan
Charles de Gaulle
Eamon De Valera
Eugene Debs
Deng Xiaoping
Benjamin Disraeli
Alexander Dubček
François & Jean-Claude
  Duvalier
Dwight Eisenhower
Eleanor of Aquitaine
Elizabeth I
Faisal
Ferdinand & Isabella
Francisco Franco
Benjamin Franklin

Frederick the Great
Indira Gandhi
Mohandas Gandhi
Giuseppe Garibaldi
Amin & Bashir Gemayel
Genghis Khan
William Gladstone
Mikhail Gorbachev
Ulysses S. Grant
Ernesto "Che" Guevara
Tenzin Gyatso
Alexander Hamilton
Dag Hammarskjöld
Henry VIII
Henry of Navarre
Paul von Hindenburg
Hirohito
Adolf Hitler
Ho Chi Minh
King Hussein
Ivan the Terrible
Andrew Jackson
James I
Wojciech Jaruzelski
Thomas Jefferson
Joan of Arc
Pope John XXIII
Pope John Paul II
Lyndon Johnson
Benito Juárez
John Kennedy
Robert Kennedy
Jomo Kenyatta
Ayatollah Khomeini
Nikita Khrushchev
Kim Il Sung
Martin Luther King, Jr.
Henry Kissinger
Kublai Khan
Lafayette
Robert E. Lee
Vladimir Lenin
Abraham Lincoln
David Lloyd George
Louis XIV
Martin Luther
Judas Maccabeus
James Madison
Nelson & Winnie
  Mandela
Mao Zedong
Ferdinand Marcos
George Marshall

Mary, Queen of Scots
Tomáš Masaryk
Golda Meir
Klemens von Metternich
James Monroe
Hosni Mubarak
Robert Mugabe
Benito Mussolini
Napoléon Bonaparte
Gamal Abdel Nasser
Jawaharlal Nehru
Nero
Nicholas II
Richard Nixon
Kwame Nkrumah
Daniel Ortega
Mohammed Reza Pahlavi
Thomas Paine
Charles Stewart
  Parnell
Pericles
Juan Perón
Peter the Great
Pol Pot
Muammar el-Qaddafi
Ronald Reagan
Cardinal Richelieu
Maximilien Robespierre
Eleanor Roosevelt
Franklin Roosevelt
Theodore Roosevelt
Anwar Sadat
Haile Selassie
Prince Sihanouk
Jan Smuts
Joseph Stalin
Sukarno
Sun Yat-sen
Tamerlane
Mother Teresa
Margaret Thatcher
Josip Broz Tito
Toussaint L'Ouverture
Leon Trotsky
Pierre Trudeau
Harry Truman
Queen Victoria
Lech Walesa
George Washington
Chaim Weizmann
Woodrow Wilson
Xerxes
Emiliano Zapata
Zhou Enlai

CHELSEA HOUSE PUBLISHERS

ON LEADERSHIP
Arthur M. Schlesinger, jr.

LEADERSHIP, it may be said, is really what makes the world go round. Love no doubt smooths the passage; but love is a private transaction between consenting adults. Leadership is a public transaction with history. The idea of leadership affirms the capacity of individuals to move, inspire, and mobilize masses of people so that they act together in pursuit of an end. Sometimes leadership serves good purposes, sometimes bad; but whether the end is benign or evil, great leaders are those men and women who leave their personal stamp on history.

Now, the very concept of leadership implies the proposition that individuals can make a difference. This proposition has never been universally accepted. From classical times to the present day, eminent thinkers have regarded individuals as no more than the agents and pawns of larger forces, whether the gods and goddesses of the ancient world or, in the modern era, race, class, nation, the dialectic, the will of the people, the spirit of the times, history itself. Against such forces, the individual dwindles into insignificance.

So contends the thesis of historical determinism. Tolstoy's great novel *War and Peace* offers a famous statement of the case. Why, Tolstoy asked, did millions of men in the Napoleonic wars, denying their human feelings and their common sense, move back and forth across Europe slaughtering their fellows? "The war," Tolstoy answered, "was bound to happen simply because it was bound to happen." All prior history predetermined it. As for leaders, they, Tolstoy said, "are but the labels that serve to give a name to an end and, like labels, they have the least possible connection with the event." The greater the leader, "the more conspicuous the inevitability and the predestination of every act he commits." The leader, said Tolstoy, is "the slave of history."

Determinism takes many forms. Marxism is the determinism of class. Nazism the determinism of race. But the idea of men and women as the slaves of history runs athwart the deepest human instincts. Rigid determinism abolishes the idea of human freedom—

the assumption of free choice that underlies every move we make, every word we speak, every thought we think. It abolishes the idea of human responsibility, since it is manifestly unfair to reward or punish people for actions that are by definition beyond their control. No one can live consistently by any deterministic creed. The Marxist states prove this themselves by their extreme susceptibility to the cult of leadership.

More than that, history refutes the idea that individuals make no difference. In December 1931 a British politician crossing Park Avenue in New York City between 76th and 77th Streets around 10:30 P.M. looked in the wrong direction and was knocked down by an automobile—a moment, he later recalled, of a man aghast, a world aglare: "I do not understand why I was not broken like an eggshell or squashed like a gooseberry." Fourteen months later an American politician, sitting in an open car in Miami, Florida, was fired on by an assassin; the man beside him was hit. Those who believe that individuals make no difference to history might well ponder whether the next two decades would have been the same had Mario Constasino's car killed Winston Churchill in 1931 and Giuseppe Zangara's bullet killed Franklin Roosevelt in 1933. Suppose, in addition, that Adolf Hitler had been killed in the street fighting during the Munich *Putsch* of 1923 and that Lenin had died of typhus during World War I. What would the 20th century be like now?

For better or for worse, individuals do make a difference. "The notion that a people can run itself and its affairs anonymously," wrote the philosopher William James, "is now well known to be the silliest of absurdities. Mankind does nothing save through initiatives on the part of inventors, great or small, and imitation by the rest of us—these are the sole factors in human progress. Individuals of genius show the way, and set the patterns, which common people then adopt and follow."

Leadership, James suggests, means leadership in thought as well as in action. In the long run, leaders in thought may well make the greater difference to the world. But, as Woodrow Wilson once said, "Those only are leaders of men, in the general eye, who lead in action. . . . It is at their hands that new thought gets its translation into the crude language of deeds." Leaders in thought often invent in solitude and obscurity, leaving to later generations the tasks of imitation. Leaders in action—the leaders portrayed in this series—have to be effective in their own time.

And they cannot be effective by themselves. They must act in response to the rhythms of their age. Their genius must be adapted, in a phrase of William James's, "to the receptivities of the moment." Leaders are useless without followers. "There goes the mob," said the French politician hearing a clamor in the streets. "I am their leader. I must follow them." Great leaders turn the inchoate emotions of the mob to purposes of their own. They seize on the opportunities of their time, the hopes, fears, frustrations, crises, potentialities. They succeed when events have prepared the way for them, when the community is awaiting to be aroused, when they can provide the clarifying and organizing ideas. Leadership ignites the circuit between the individual and the mass and thereby alters history.

It may alter history for better or for worse. Leaders have been responsible for the most extravagant follies and most monstrous crimes that have beset suffering humanity. They have also been vital in such gains as humanity has made in individual freedom, religious and racial tolerance, social justice and respect for human rights.

There is no sure way to tell in advance who is going to lead for good and who for evil. But a glance at the gallery of men and women in *World Leaders—Past and Present* suggests some useful tests.

One test is this: do leaders lead by force or by persuasion? By command or by consent? Through most of history leadership was exercised by the divine right of authority. The duty of followers was to defer and to obey. "Theirs not to reason why,/ Theirs but to do and die." On occasion, as with the so-called "enlightened despots" of the 18th century in Europe, absolutist leadership was animated by humane purposes. More often, absolutism nourished the passion for domination, land, gold and conquest and resulted in tyranny.

The great revolution of modern times has been the revolution of equality. The idea that all people should be equal in their legal condition has undermined the old structure of authority, hierarchy and deference. The revolution of equality has had two contrary effects on the nature of leadership. For equality, as Alexis de Tocqueville pointed out in his great study *Democracy in America*, might mean equality in servitude as well as equality in freedom.

"I know of only two methods of establishing equality in the political world," Tocqueville wrote. "Rights must be given to every citizen, or none at all to anyone . . . save one, who is the master of all." There was no middle ground "between the sovereignty of all and the absolute power of one man." In his astonishing prediction of 20th-century totalitarian dictatorship, Tocqueville explained how the revolution of equality could lead to the *"Führerprinzip"* and more terrible absolutism than the world had ever known.

But when rights are given to every citizen and the sovereignty of all is established, the problem of leadership takes a new form, becomes more exacting than ever before. It is easy to issue commands and enforce them by the rope and the stake, the concentration camp and the *gulag.* It is much harder to use argument and achievement to overcome opposition and win consent. The Founding Fathers of the United States understood the difficulty. They believed that history had given them the opportunity to decide, as Alexander Hamilton wrote in the first Federalist Paper, whether men are indeed capable of basing government on "reflection and choice, or whether they are forever destined to depend . . . on accident and force."

Government by reflection and choice called for a new style of leadership and a new quality of followership. It required leaders to be responsive to popular concerns, and it required followers to be active and informed participants in the process. Democracy does not eliminate emotion from politics; sometimes it fosters demagoguery; but it is confident that, as the greatest of democratic leaders put it, you cannot fool all of the people all of the time. It measures leadership by results and retires those who overreach or falter or fail.

It is true that in the long run despots are measured by results too. But they can postpone the day of judgment, sometimes indefinitely, and in the meantime they can do infinite harm. It is also true that democracy is no guarantee of virtue and intelligence in government, for the voice of the people is not necessarily the voice of God. But democracy, by assuring the right of opposition, offers built-in resistance to the evils inherent in absolutism. As the theologian Reinhold Niebuhr summed it up, "Man's capacity for justice makes democracy possible, but man's inclination to injustice makes democracy necessary."

A second test for leadership is the end for which power is sought. When leaders have as their goal the supremacy of a master race or the promotion of totalitarian revolution or the acquisition and exploitation of colonies or the protection of greed and privilege or the preservation of personal power, it is likely that their leadership will do little to advance the cause of humanity. When their goal is the abolition of slavery, the liberation of women, the enlargement of opportunity for the poor and powerless, the extension of equal rights to racial minorities, the defense of the freedoms of expression and opposition, it is likely that their leadership will increase the sum of human liberty and welfare.

Leaders have done great harm to the world. They have also conferred great benefits. You will find both sorts in this series. Even "good" leaders must be regarded with a certain wariness. Leaders are not demigods; they put on their trousers one leg after another just like ordinary mortals. No leader is infallible, and every leader needs to be reminded of this at regular intervals. Irreverence irritates leaders but is their salvation. Unquestioning submission corrupts leaders and demands followers. Making a cult of a leader is always a mistake. Fortunately hero worship generates its own antidote. "Every hero," said Emerson, "becomes a bore at last."

The signal benefit the great leaders confer is to embolden the rest of us to live according to our own best selves, to be active, insistent, and resolute in affirming our own sense of things. For great leaders attest to the reality of human freedom against the supposed inevitabilities of history. And they attest to the wisdom and power that may lie within the most unlikely of us, which is why Abraham Lincoln remains the supreme example of great leadership. A great leader, said Emerson, exhibits new possibilities to all humanity. "We feed on genius. . . . Great men exist that there may be greater men."

Great leaders, in short, justify themselves by emancipating and empowering their followers. So humanity struggles to master its destiny, remembering with Alexis de Tocqueville: "It is true that around every man a fatal circle is traced beyond which he cannot pass; but within the wide verge of that circle he is powerful and free; as it is with man, so with communities."

1

Tragedy in Dallas

On Tuesday, November 19, 1963, Vice-president Lyndon B. Johnson arrived at his Texas homestead to check preparations for two house guests expected that weekend at the LBJ Ranch: President John F. Kennedy and his wife, Jacqueline. Poland Spring Water and Ballantine's scotch were purchased for the president's pleasure; champagne and Salem cigarettes for the First Lady's. Phones were installed throughout the house, carefully placed for the president's convenience, but tucked away inconspicuously so as not to divert him from the main object of his visit, a full day of relaxation. The president's stay at the LBJ Ranch was to conclude a two-day swing through Texas that would lay the groundwork for Kennedy's reelection campaign in 1964.

But as Johnson surveyed the arrangements and pronounced himself pleased with the results, he had no way of knowing the president would never arrive. Three days later, an assassin's bullet would make Vice-president Lyndon B. Johnson the 36th president of the United States. Johnson had become a popular figure in Texas politics over the course of three decades in Congress, rising through the ranks

The greatest shock that I can recall was one of the men saying, "He's gone."
—LYNDON JOHNSON
on his reaction to John F. Kennedy's death

Virtually all Americans born before 1957 remember where they were when they heard that President Kennedy had been assassinated. With no time for mourning, Vice-president Johnson was sworn into the highest office in the land.

Johnson and his wife, known as Lady Bird, stand in front of their home on the LBJ Ranch near Stonewall, Texas. The couple would always return to the ranch to rest and entertain close friends throughout Johnson's political career.

of the Senate to become majority leader, the top position in the upper chamber. Through his mastery of Texas politics and the intricacies of the Senate, Johnson acquired something of a national following as a moderate in the Democratic party, known for his ability to build a consensus and get things done.

In 1960 Johnson had run for president. The campaign for the nomination of the Democratic party narrowed down to Johnson and Senator Kennedy of Massachusetts. Kennedy emerged the winner. The campaign was hard fought, but the two candidates developed a mutual admiration over the course of it. Kennedy chose Johnson to be his vice-presidential nominee. Recognizing Johnson's popularity in his home state, Kennedy left the campaign in Texas to his running mate. Johnson stumped brilliantly for the ticket, crisscrossing the state time and again. His efforts paid off in a narrow victory for the liberal Kennedy in conservative Texas. The votes Johnson garnered in Texas were crucial to Kennedy's victory over Republican nominee Richard Nixon in one of the closest presidential elections in history.

But many voters in the South, including those in Texas, opposed the Kennedy administration's liberal policies. In Johnson's absence, liberals and conservatives in the state Democratic party had begun feuding in rough-and-tumble Texas fashion. Kennedy and Johnson hoped a swing through the state would shore up the administration's popularity and reunite the squabbling factions for the upcoming election.

Their hopes seemed well founded on Friday morning, November 22, when Johnson brought his sister, Lucia Alexander, to meet President Kennedy in his suite at the Hotel Texas in Fort Worth. The president was in high spirits. Large and enthusiastic crowds had greeted Kennedy in San Antonio and Houston the day before. Despite some hostile remarks in the conservative press, the trip seemed to be going well. "We're going to carry two states next year if we don't carry any others," Kennedy told Johnson confidently. "Texas and Massachusetts."

"Oh, we're going to do better than that, Mr. President," Johnson replied. They were the last words Vice-president Lyndon B. Johnson would ever speak to President John F. Kennedy.

Air Force One touched down in Dallas at 11:40 A.M. under a clear sky and a bright sun. Standing at the head of the receiving line on the tarmac of Love Field, Johnson was struck by how radiant Jacqueline Kennedy looked in a pink suit and hat as she stepped from the plane. Taking her hand, Johnson shrugged boyishly at the strained formality of their fourth airport greeting in 24 hours. The receiving line followed the Kennedys to a crowd of about a thousand Texans waiting to greet the First Family, Johnson, and his wife, Lady Bird. After shaking hands and greeting old friends, the Johnsons took their place in the motorcade that would wind through downtown Dallas.

The motorcade pulled out from Love Field at 11:55 A.M., led by the presidential limousine carrying Governor John Connally of Texas and his wife in the front seat and the Kennedys in the back. A Secret Service car and the vice-presidential limousine carrying Lyndon and Lady Bird Johnson and Texas senator Ralph Yarborough followed closely behind.

John Kennedy and his wife, Jacqueline, with their daughter, Caroline, at the family compound in Hyannis Port, Massachusetts, in 1960. The Kennedy family brought a youth and vibrancy to the White House that made the nation's grief at JFK's assassination particularly intense.

Following the assassination of her husband, Jacqueline Kennedy watches as the president's body is taken to Bethesda Naval Hospital. She is accompanied by the president's brother Attorney General Robert Kennedy (to the left of Jacqueline).

The president stopped the motorcade twice as it made its way up Alto Drive, first for a group of children holding a placard saying MR. PRESIDENT, PLEASE STOP AND SHAKE OUR HANDS, and later to greet a group of nuns. As the motorcade approached the center of town, the crowds lining Live Oak Street and the affection shown the president grew. The smiling children waving signs, and the people hanging out of office windows cheering and pouring confetti down upon the motorcade convinced Johnson that the president was right in predicting they would carry Texas in 1964.

At 12:30 P.M., the motorcade turned right off Main Street onto Houston Street, then left onto Elm, which would lead to an underpass and then onto Stemmons Freeway. Just as the vice-presidential car turned onto Elm Street, Johnson was startled by what sounded like an explosion coming from the back of the motorcade. Before he could turn to see what it was, Secret Service agent Rufus Youngblood spun around from the front seat and pushed the vice-president down to the floor of the car.

With Youngblood sitting on his shoulder, Johnson craned his neck to his right to make sure that Lady Bird and Senator Yarborough were unhurt. Then he heard another explosion shake the air. A Secret Service radio squawked from the front seat. The limousine accelerated so suddenly up over a curb and around a corner that it seemed to Johnson as if the car were riding on two wheels. As the motorcade sped past the Trade Mart where President Kennedy was scheduled to deliver a speech, Youngblood told the vice-president that they were going to a hospital. Crouching in the back seat, Johnson heard Youngblood speak into the crackling radio several times. "When we get to the hospital," Youngblood told Johnson, "you and Mrs. Johnson follow me and the other agents."

The car stopped a moment later. A phalanx of agents surrounded the Johnsons as they got out of the car, and walked them quickly into the hospital. Their appearance at the hospital kindled a rumor that the vice-president had suffered a heart attack. In the frenzied moments that followed, as the eyes of the nation fastened upon Parkland Hospital, the press would circulate the rumor throughout the country.

Johnson, of course, knew they had not come to the hospital for his benefit. He realized that the explosion he had heard in the motorcade must have been gunfire. But as he and Lady Bird waited in a small room in the hospital, he did not know who had been injured in the shooting. Emory Roberts, the Secret Service agent in charge of the White House, was the first to inform Johnson that President Kennedy had been seriously wounded and that Governor Connally had been injured. Johnson would later recall that he was stunned at the news about "my president and leader" and Connally, "my confidant and friend." In a single moment, Johnson thought, "the day, which had started out so cheerfully, had turned into a nightmare."

The Secret Service, unsure whether the shooting was the act of a single gunman or part of a larger plot, decided that Johnson should leave Dallas immediately. "The White House will be the safest place

I knew, of course, that I was on my own and that it was my responsibility and it was a thing that had to be dealt with very quickly and as calmly as could be. And I tried to think it out, recognize the problems that faced me and the necessity of giving the nation and the world confidence as soon as I could.
—LYNDON JOHNSON
after assuming
the presidency

Johnson took the oath of office aboard *Air Force One*, the presidential plane, after the Kennedy assassination. The president's grieving widow stands beside him.

for you," Youngblood explained. Johnson, however, wanted to stay with President Kennedy.

During the next 45 minutes Johnson waited in a state of shock for further news about Kennedy and Connally. Lady Bird and Cliff Carter, an aide to the vice-president, stayed with Johnson throughout those tense moments. Secret Service agents and several Texas congressmen filed in and out. Kenneth O'Donnell, President Kennedy's chief aide, came in to say that the president was "in a bad way." Emory Roberts, the Secret Service agent, returned to say that the president would not survive. But another Secret Service agent said later that the president was being taken into surgery and that he would recover.

At 1:20 P.M., O'Donnell returned. "He's gone," O'Donnell said. Johnson thought back to how young and vigorous John F. Kennedy had been in their final visit just hours before. The president could not be dead, Johnson thought. But President Kennedy was dead. The first explosion Johnson had heard while in the motorcade was a rifle shot; the bullet had entered the back of Kennedy's neck, torn his windpipe, and exited through his throat. The same bullet continued through Connally's back, chest, right wrist, and left thigh. Had the attack been limited to that single shot, Kennedy might have survived, as did Connally. But the second explosion Johnson heard was from the discharge of a second bullet that found its mark in the back of the president's head, killing him almost instantly.

At about half past one, Malcolm Kilduff, President Kennedy's assistant press secretary, entered the room and turned to Lyndon Johnson. "Mr. President," Kilduff began, "I have to announce the death of President Kennedy. Is it all right with you if I make the announcement now?" It was the first time anyone had addressed him as "Mr. President," and the words struck Johnson as strange and startling. He later recalled that "in spite of my sense of personal loss and deep shock, I knew I could not allow the tide of grief to overwhelm me. The consequences of my actions were too great for me to become immobilized now with emotion. I was a man in trouble, in a world that is never more than minutes away from catastrophe." Lyndon Baines Johnson was president of the United States.

Thousands of mourners line the streets of Washington for Kennedy's funeral procession in November 1963. Johnson vowed to devote the remainder of the term to completing Kennedy's unfinished agenda.

2

A Hill Country Youth

Lyndon Johnson was 55 years old when he took the oath of office aboard *Air Force One*. Although Johnson wanted the presidency badly enough to run for it in 1960, he had never wanted to be the beneficiary of an assassin's bullet. Nonetheless, the tragedy in Dallas was the final step in a remarkable political career that had begun 30 years before, in the depths of the Great Depression. Johnson was only 23 years old when he went to Washington as secretary to a freshman congressman, and only 29 when he became a congressman himself. In 1948 he was elected to the Senate, and he quickly rose through the ranks to become majority leader in 1955. Johnson's extraordinary rise was all the more remarkable for its humble beginnings in the hill country of southwestern Texas.

There was little in the circumstances of Lyndon Johnson's childhood to suggest he would ever be president, yet Lyndon was, in a sense, a born politician. His family had always had big dreams and an interest in politics. The Johnsons could trace their roots back to John Wheeler Bunton, who signed Texas's Declaration of Independence from Mexico in 1835. His grandfather Samuel Ealy Johnson ran for the state legislature in 1892. And his father, Samuel Ealy Johnson, Jr., represented the hill country in the Texas House of Representatives for 10 years.

He was never content long to play quietly in the yard. He must take his toys apart to see what made them go . . . to conquer that new unexplored world beyond the gate or up the lane.
—REBEKAH BAINES
Johnson's mother,
on Johnson's
childhood curiosity

Lyndon Johnson at 18 months. He was an extremely precocious child who — thanks to his mother's tutoring — knew the alphabet by the age of two and was reading at four.

Lyndon's paternal grandfather, Sam Johnson, was one of the most successful cattlemen in Texas. In 1870, he and his wife, Eliza Bunton, and his brother, Tom, drove 7,000 longhorns nearly 700 miles north to Abilene, Kansas. They returned carrying sacks filled with gold, but their success was brief. A drought wiped out the Johnson brothers' herd in 1872, taking their entire fortune with it.

In 1877, Sam and Eliza had a son, Sam Ealy Johnson, Jr. The family moved to a 100-acre farm in Buda, bought with money given to them by Eliza's father. Farming was difficult in the rocky soil of the hill country, and crop prices were plummeting. Sam Johnson rarely received more than $600 for his entire crop.

Sam was not alone in his difficulties. Farmers all over western Texas were going into debt and losing their farms. Then, in the 1880s, a "populist" movement swept through Texas. The populists believed that the railroad companies, bankers, and big corporations were cheating farmers out of a fair price for the supplies they needed to buy, the money they needed to borrow, and the crops they needed to sell. The populists banded together in cooperatives that allowed them to buy their supplies and sell their crops at better prices.

The cooperatives helped, but by the 1890s the populists knew they could not get the credit and crop prices they needed to survive without government help. They started a nationwide Populist party to elect representatives to the state legislatures and the Congress who would fight the "big interests." When Sam Johnson ran for the Texas state legislature in 1892, he ran as a Populist firebrand. Johnson lost the election, but he passed on his populist idealism to his son, Sam, Jr.

In 1904, at the age of 27, Sam, Jr., was elected to the Texas House of Representatives. The Populist party no longer existed by then, but Sam, Jr., remained a populist. The big interests remained as powerful as ever. To make sure the representatives remembered who their friends were when the interests needed a special law passed, business lobbyists used to do favors for representatives, buying them drinks, meals, and even women. But Sam never took anything from the interests. Texas politicians used to say that Sam Ealy Johnson, Jr., was "straight as a shingle."

Before Sam, Jr., the hill country's representative in the House had been Joseph Wilson Baines. Baines came from a long line of Baptist preachers. He was a religious man who cared deeply about nature and literature. Baines was a distinguished citizen — a former newspaper publisher and secretary of state under Governor John Ireland of Texas. In 1904 a drought threw Baines's farm holdings into bankruptcy. He retired from the House and died in 1906. His wife took in boarders to make ends meet, and his daughter, Rebekah, worked part-time for an Austin newspaper to earn enough money to finish school at Baylor University. Before her father died, he suggested she interview the young man who had won his seat in the House.

She finally interviewed Sam Ealy Johnson, Jr., in 1907. She later said that she found him difficult to pin down but thought him "dashing and dynamic." She was captivated by his "flashing eyes" and happy to have found a man she could talk to about "principles," as she had to her father.

Sam was happy, too, because he had found a woman as romantic and idealistic as himself. Slender, with blond hair and blue eyes, she also shared his interest in politics. They began what Rebekah later called a "whirlwind courtship." Sam would ride 20 miles to visit her in Fredericksburg, where she taught elocution, and take her to hear speeches by the great orators of Texas politics.

On August 20, 1907, after only a few months, they were married. They moved to a small house with two rooms separated by a breezeway. Behind one room was a kitchen, and behind the other was a porch overlooking a long slope that led down to a muddy stretch of the Pedernales River. Managing a household in those days was difficult, and Rebekah had never done it before. Just washing clothes was an ordeal. Enormous vats had to be filled with water hauled up from the river and boiled over a wood-burning stove. Heavy with water, the clothes had to be scrubbed for hours with home-made soap.

Lyndon's mother, the former Rebekah Baines. As a young reporter she interviewed Sam Johnson for an Austin newspaper. Several months later, after a whirlwind courtship, the couple was married.

Sam decided not to run for reelection to his seat in the legislature in 1908 — he had decided he would earn a living farming cotton, as his father had. He was paid very little as a legislator, he was several thousand dollars in debt, and besides, he and Rebekah had a family now.

Lyndon was born on August 27, 1908. Rebekah had high hopes for the boy and was determined that he get a good education. She began tutoring him at an early age, telling him stories from the Bible and teaching him mythology and history as well. By the time he was two, he had learned the alphabet. Lyndon could read at the age of four.

He was a curious and energetic child. It seemed that the moment Rebekah turned her back, Lyndon had run off somewhere. It happened so frequently that Sam hung a cowbell on the front porch to make it easier for Rebekah to summon him from the fields to mount a search for Lyndon. Often they would find him down the road at the Junction School, playing with the children who were already old enough to go to school every day. After a while, Sam and Rebekah stopped bringing Lyndon back from the school and started sending him there each morning with the older children.

When Lyndon was five, the family moved to a larger house in nearby Johnson City. Lyndon already had two sisters by that time, and a brother, Sam Houston, was born a few months later.

In Johnson City, Lyndon began to show an uncanny ability to make himself the center of attention. He no longer had to run away to find playmates. There were many children in Johnson City. Most of Lyndon's friends were 5 and even 10 years older than he. He had no trouble, however, keeping up with them — he even held his own in poker games. But Lyndon was more than just one of the gang — he was the ringleader among the older children. They found that Lyndon seemed to speak and think faster than they did. When they got into trouble, they relied on Lyndon to talk their way out of it.

Soon Lyndon's companions were not just older children but grown men. When Lyndon was 10, he got a job shining shoes at Cecil Maddox's barbershop, where the men of Johnson City gathered to talk politics. The barbershop received the only newspaper to be found in Johnson City, and Lyndon always made sure he was the first to read it. He liked to climb up in a barber's chair and read the paper aloud to the assembled adults, commenting about the news as he read it. Sometimes the older men disagreed with Lyndon's remarks, but Lyndon always disagreed right back.

Lyndon had learned how to debate at his parents' dinner table. During dinner Sam Johnson would ask his children questions about political issues, such as whether the United States should join the League of Nations or whether the government should take over the railroads from the big interests. Sam had strong opinions on these matters (he was in favor of both), but he never insisted his children agree with him. He did insist that they have opinions, though, and that they be able to defend them.

Lyndon's father was reelected to his seat in the state House of Representatives in 1917. Politicians often came to talk with Sam on the porch outside

Lyndon Johnson's father, Sam Ealy Johnson, Jr., was a member of the Texas House of Representatives for 10 years. Sam often took his son to the state legislature and out on the campaign trail.

Lyndon's room. Lyndon was too young to join these discussions, so he would go into his room, open his window, and listen to the politicians plan strategy, debate the issues, or tell stories about the great men of Texas politics. On the Fourth of July in 1918 Governor William P. Hobby came to the Johnson home for dinner. The house was crowded with politicians from all over Texas. To make room for the guests, Lyndon was supposed to eat in the kitchen, but he hid under the dinner table to make sure he heard every word of the conversation.

That same year Lyndon's father took him to the state legislature in Austin for the first time. Lyndon began to imitate his father, wearing a big Stetson hat and walking with a long strut. Lyndon also imitated his father's unique way of speaking. Looking intently into the eyes of a fellow representative, Sam Johnson would bend down, putting his arm around his colleague's shoulders. If his colleague continued to disagree, Johnson grabbed him by the lapels of his coat to emphasize his point. Lyndon liked to talk to his father's colleagues, and soon he, too, was bending down into their faces, putting his arm around their shoulders, and tugging at their lapels for emphasis. During Lyndon Johnson's years in Washington, this unique method of persuasion would become his trademark.

Lyndon Johnson would later say that he had never been happier than when he accompanied his father on political trips. "I loved going with my father to the legislature. I would sit in the gallery for hours watching all the activity on the floor and then would wander around the halls trying to figure out what was going on. The only thing I loved more was going with him on the trail during his campaigns for reelection."

Lyndon's father earned a comfortable living, supplementing his legislator's salary with income from his farm and real-estate deals. Yet he could never save the money he earned, buying new clothes or a new car with whatever spare cash he had. When his parents died, he sold everything he owned to buy their 400-acre farm on the Pedernales. Shortly after, the price of cotton fell sharply and he had to sell the farm for much less than he had paid for it. He moved his family back to Johnson City when Lyndon was 14 and got part-time work as a game warden and additional employment in a series of other public-works jobs. His health deteriorated, and he decided not to run for reelection in 1924.

Sam Ealy Johnson, Jr., had never been rich, but his children always had enough to eat, and they were always a little better dressed than their friends. But by the time Lyndon turned 16, this was no longer true. His father was often sick and unable to work. He accumulated large debts to local merchants. When they refused to give him more credit, he went to merchants in other towns and got credit from them. The Johnsons often depended on neighbors to bring them food.

Lyndon had a difficult time adjusting to the family's new circumstances. He had idolized his father. But now he seemed to hear whispers about his father's debts wherever he went. Lyndon's relationship with his father, once so adoring, now became adversarial. He refused to listen to his father. He ignored his chores, and he frequently sneaked out of the house late at night to go out with his friends.

Lyndon's parents were particularly upset that Lyndon neglected his schoolwork. They believed that without a college education Lyndon would be trapped in the hill country, which offered few opportunities besides the hard life of farming. But in rejecting his parents' authority, Lyndon had also rejected the value they placed on education. When Lyndon graduated from high school, he refused to go to college no matter how much his parents pleaded with him to change his mind.

The summer after he graduated, Lyndon worked building a highway between Johnson City and Aus-

> *With the physique he had plus his acting ability he could be a terrible bully. He would shake his hand under your nose, stride up and down, raise his arms. He knew exactly what he was doing.*
> —ELIZABETH GOLDSCHMIDT
> vice-president, Crusade Against Poverty, on Johnson's arguing technique

Lyndon Johnson was born in this house in Stonewall, Texas, on August 27, 1908. He would later build the LBJ Ranch only 400 yards away.

tin. It was backbreaking work in the hot Texas sun and paid only two dollars a day, but that was all the work there was in the hill country. After wrecking his father's car one night, Lyndon ran away to Robstown, more than 100 miles south of Austin, and found work in a cotton gin. Lyndon agreed to come home only after his father promised never to mention the wrecked car.

Young people from the hill country looking for opportunities often found them in California. In the fall, Lyndon and a group of friends piled into a Model T Ford and headed west. Lyndon's cousin Tom Martin, an attorney in San Bernardino, offered Lyndon and his friend Fritz Koeninger jobs in his law office. Lyndon wanted to be a lawyer, but he could not join the California bar without a college education. However, he did not need a college degree to join the bar in Nevada. Tom suggested that Lyndon study his law books at night and take the bar examination to become a lawyer in Nevada. After he was admitted to the Nevada bar, Lyndon could join the bar in California and practice law with Tom. Lyndon agreed, and he began studying at night and working in Tom's office during the day.

The Johnson children in 1921. From left to right: Lucia, Josepha, Rebekah, Lyndon, Sam Houston.

At first Lyndon ran errands for Tom, filed his papers, and typed his letters. But each day Tom seemed to be turning more and more of his work over to Lyndon and Fritz. As Tom spent less time in the office, Fritz and Lyndon began advising his clients as if they were real lawyers. Lyndon continued studying for the Nevada bar exam, and it seemed he would soon be a lawyer himself. His future seemed bright, and, most important to Lyndon, he was succeeding without going to college.

After a year in Tom's office, however, everything changed. Lyndon realized that the advice he was giving to Tom's clients actually meant he was practicing law without a license. This was a serious matter. Practicing law without a license was illegal, and Lyndon could go to jail for it. In addition, Nevada was making it more difficult to join the bar, and Johnson realized he could not become a lawyer as easily as Tom had promised.

In the fall of 1925, Lyndon returned to Johnson City, deeply disappointed and a little shaken by the year he had spent in California. He returned to the road gang and stayed there for over a year. His parents always said he would never get anywhere in life without a college education. Lyndon was beginning to think they were right. Two years out of high school, he was back where he had started. He had refused to go to college and had gone to California to escape the road gang. Now he was back on the road gang, doing the same backbreaking work from six in the morning until six at night. In the winter of 1927, Lyndon told his parents he was ready to go to college.

When Lyndon was five, the family moved to this spacious home in Johnson City, Texas. He now had two sisters and a baby brother on the way.

29

3

"A Remarkable Young Man"

The only college in the 24,000 square miles of the hill country was Southwest Texas State Teachers College in San Marcos. The San Marcos campus consisted of four buildings set on the highest hill in the town, so that the four spires of the main building could be seen from miles away. It was hardly the best college education America had to offer, but it was all that most of its students, including Lyndon Johnson, could afford.

Cecil "Prexy" Evans, president of San Marcos, was a dour man who rarely looked up from the little black book he always seemed to be writing in as he walked around the campus. Even faculty members could rarely get more than a few words out of Evans. But Lyndon had a way with older men. He found that President Evans had an avid interest in government. In fact, the notes he was always scribbling were often about politics. President Evans rarely stopped to talk with anyone because no one at San Marcos knew enough about politics to have an interesting conversation about it. But Lyndon Johnson did. President Evans took an interest in this young man who seemed to know stories about every politician in Texas.

To lead inquiring and impressionable minds into the great treasure house of knowledge that the world has accumulated is of itself a priceless privilege. To be of service to humanity is recompense for struggling years and patient study.
—LYNDON JOHNSON
on his commitment
to education

Johnson on his 18th birthday, the year before he entered Southwest Texas State Teachers College. A year of work on a highway road gang helped convince Johnson that a college degree was essential to his future.

Most of the students at San Marcos needed jobs to stay in school, but employment was often difficult to find. When Lyndon told the president he needed to earn more money to stay in school, he gave Lyndon a coveted job mopping the floors of Old Main, the administration building, for 30 cents an hour. Soon Lyndon was working in the president's office as an assistant to his personal secretary. Later in the semester Lyndon became the president's appointments secretary and often accompanied Evans to Austin when he had to go before the legislature.

Lyndon did not have enough money to pay for his second year at San Marcos, so he took a job teaching at a school in Cotulla, 60 miles northeast of the Mexican border. At Welhausen Ward Elementary School most of the students were Mexicans. Welhausen had never had athletics or extracurricular activities, as the local school for white children had. But Lyndon persuaded the school board to provide equipment for a volleyball and a softball team. Soon Welhausen was hosting track meets and baseball games the way other schools did. Lyndon also took

The students of Welhausen Ward Elementary School, where Johnson taught from 1928 to 1929, were mostly Mexicans from poor families. Johnson (top, center) organized their first athletic program.

the children's education more seriously than the other teachers did. He insisted that the students speak English at all times. He even organized assemblies for the entire school in which the students performed skits and held debates. He arranged spelling bees and public-speaking contests with other schools.

His year in Cotulla was a great success. But it had been a very lonely time for him, too. The other teachers all had their own families, and Lyndon spent most of his free time alone. He was happy to return to San Marcos in the summer of 1929. School was not then in session, but Lyndon stayed on campus to be editor of *The Star*, the college newspaper. He had hoped to stay on as editor during the school year. The students elected him editorial writer instead.

Lyndon was not as popular among his fellow students as he was with the faculty at San Marcos. In fact, it was his popularity with the faculty that many of the students did not like. They thought he tried too hard to ingratiate himself with President Evans and his teachers. He also could be very overbearing with people his own age, boasting about his skills as a debater and about all the politicians he knew and the girlfriends he had.

Actually, Lyndon did not have a girlfriend at San Marcos. He was a tall, handsome young man with black hair, dark eyes, and delicate features, but he was a little awkward. The most attractive women at San Marcos all dated members of the "Black Stars," a not-so-secret secret society of athletes who met on a big meadow on a nearby farm to drink beer. As the most popular men on campus, the Black Stars ran the student government and the school paper and got the best campus jobs.

Lyndon tried to join the Black Stars, but they would not have him. He and his friends thought they would have more luck with the San Marcos women if they had their own secret society. So Johnson started his own society, the White Stars. The pretty girls all seemed perfectly happy with their Black Stars, but Lyndon realized many students were not very pleased with the way the Black Stars ran the student government.

> *Somehow you never forget what poverty and hatred can do when you see its scars on the hopeful face of a young child.*
> —LYNDON JOHNSON
> impression after teaching in Cotulla, Texas, at a Mexican-American school

33

The student council's main task was to decide how funds for extracurricular activities were spent. Most of the students were not athletes, but very little money was allocated to the activities nonathletes might enjoy, such as debate and drama. Lyndon organized a campaign to elect Bill Deason student council president on the slogan "Brains are just as important as Brawn."

Lyndon worked frenetically to get Deason elected. Every night Lyndon went down to the boarding-houses where San Marcos students lived, asking them to vote for Bill Deason. As Lyndon explained to them one-by-one that Deason would make sure the nonathletes got their fair share of student-activity funds, he bent down into their faces and put his arm around their shoulders, just as his father had in Austin. Thanks to Lyndon's efforts, Bill Deason won the election. The following year Lyndon became president of the senior class. President Evans told the deans to consult with Lyndon when they assigned campus jobs. And although Lyndon was running short of cash, he never got an "inside job" for himself. By the time he graduated from San Marcos in the summer of 1930, the White Stars had control of the student publications, the student government, and the best campus jobs. He had also earned the respect of many students who had once disliked him.

Jobless men and women stand in line for bread during the Great Depression. Scenes like this were common throughout the country during the 1930s.

Lyndon was by no means the best student at San Marcos. He graduated with a B.S. degree with a B-average and managed that only with his mother's help. But Lyndon's years at San Marcos had taught him many of the skills that would be central to his later success. His ability to see the political potential of a social organization such as the White Stars would come in very handy when he went to Washington as a congressional secretary. The same energy he showed in getting Bill Deason elected president of the student council would eventually make Lyndon a congressman. And it would not be long before the skill that Lyndon had shown in currying the favor of President Cecil Evans would make him a favorite of President Franklin Roosevelt.

But first Lyndon had to get to Washington, D.C. Just before he graduated from San Marcos, he attended a "speaking" with his parents, where Welly K. Hopkins, a young state representative heard Lyndon give an impromptu speech. Hopkins was impressed and asked Lyndon to help him on his reelection campaign. Through one of his White Star friends, Lyndon got a mimeograph machine and stationery to run off campaign flyers. He also enlisted the White Stars to campaign for Hopkins in small towns. Hopkins won by a large margin and gave Lyndon most of the credit.

Franklin D. Roosevelt (center, right) was elected president in 1932. Roosevelt promised a New Deal in his inaugural address to ease the suffering caused by the depression and assured Americans that the only thing they had to fear was "fear itself."

After teaching for a year at Sam Houston High School, Lyndon got a call from Richard M. Kleberg, who had just been elected to Congress from Texas's 14th District. Kleberg needed a secretary, and Hopkins had spoken very highly of young Johnson. Would Lyndon come to Washington D.C., with him as his aide? Lyndon had enjoyed teaching, but he was eager to get into politics. Lyndon joined Kleberg five days later for the trip to Washington.

Lyndon was only 23 when he and Congressman Kleberg arrived in the capital on December 7, 1931. Congressman Kleberg was only a freshman, and freshmen congressmen had very little power. Furthermore, as the son of one of the wealthiest ranchers in Texas, Kleberg had never worked very hard, and he had no intention of changing his habits just because he had been elected to the U.S. House of Representatives. He rarely came to his office on Capitol Hill before noon, and he frequently never came in at all.

Lyndon knew that the key to staying elected for a freshman congressman was to stay in touch with the voters back home, helping smooth out their problems with government agencies. Mail arrived three times a day, and Lyndon insisted that his two assistants answer each letter by the end of the day. Lyndon could rarely get Congressman Kleberg to read the mail, much less dictate a reply or telephone a government agency on a constituent's behalf. Lyndon would have to figure out for himself how to get things done in Washington.

Fortunately, he lived with several other secretaries in the basement of a hotel at the foot of Capitol Hill. They were ambitious young men with a keen interest in politics and the ways of Washington. When the secretaries swapped opinions and information, Lyndon would question them about how they got things done. And he kept asking questions until he was sure he had found the secret of their success.

Lyndon and his two assistants would arrive at the office before daybreak and leave after nightfall. Lyndon allowed no weekends off for Congressman Kleberg's staff: They worked seven days a week. The Great Depression was deepening, and the stacks of

Representative Richard Kleberg, in Texan dress, entertains servicemen at the Stage Door Canteen in Washington. Kleberg gave Johnson his first job in politics, as a congressional secretary.

mail grew higher and higher with requests for jobs, new government programs, or the congressman's help in securing benefits for veterans. When constituents had problems with the Veterans Administration, Lyndon quickly found the right person to call. If that did not work, he would go to the VA himself, file an appeal, and secure a lawyer for the constituent.

When Franklin D. Roosevelt became president in 1933, he began a series of programs called the New Deal, which created government jobs for the unemployed and offered farmers the kind of government aid that populists had been seeking for decades.

One New Deal agency, the Agricultural Adjustment Administration, tried to raise crop prices by paying farmers to plant fewer crops. But farmers were suspicious of a government program that paid them *not* to plant crops. Lyndon telephoned county agents of the AAA, hounding them to sign up more farmers and suggesting how they might convince farmers to join the program. Applications had to go through several bureaus in the AAA. Lyndon often appeared at the agency to usher applications through its complex bureaucracy. When the government warned that so few farmers had joined the program it might have to be canceled, Congressman Kleberg's 14th District had already surpassed its quota. President Roosevelt presented the first check issued under the program to a farmer from the 14th District.

In 1919, the Little Congress was founded to give congressional secretaries experience in public speaking and legislative procedure. By the time Lyndon arrived on Capitol Hill, it had become little more than a social club for a dozen secretaries. But Lyndon saw bigger possibilities for the Little Congress, just as he had seen the political potential of the White Stars at San Marcos.

In 1933, when the Little Congress held elections for a new Speaker, Lyndon was thought to have little chance of winning. He had been a secretary for only two years, and seniority was the key to moving ahead in the Little Congress, just as it was in the

I would not say I was without ambition ever. . . . To realize that the people you were passing were probably congressmen . . . maybe senators, members of the cabinet. And there was the smell of power. It's got an odor . . . power I mean.
—LYNDON JOHNSON
on arriving in Washington, D.C.

Senator Huey Long of Louisiana was a controversial figure during the 1930s, his renown linked to populist notions of redistributing the wealth in order to make "every man a king." He was assassinated in 1935.

real Congress. But Lyndon organized other Capitol Hill employees — postal workers, guards, elevator operators — who were also eligible to vote but rarely did. Lyndon won the election and quickly turned the Little Congress into an important political organization. He held meetings more frequently. He met important legislators such as Senator Tom Connally and Senator Huey Long by inviting them to speak at the meetings. He had the Little Congress debate upcoming legislation. Reporters began covering the debates because the secretaries often reflected the positions of the congressmen they worked for. Soon congressmen were asking Lyndon to have their bills debated in the Little Congress.

But Lyndon wanted to be a member of the real Congress. He hoped working for Richard Kleberg would put him in a good position to run for the congressman's seat when he tired of life in Washington. By 1934, however, it was clear that Kleberg had no plans to retire in the near future. Lyndon was frustrated that his hard work had brought him no closer to becoming a congressman.

Lyndon met Claudia Alta Taylor that same year. The daughter of one of the wealthiest men in Karnack, Texas, Claudia was nicknamed Lady Bird because, as her nurse said, Claudia was "pretty as a lady bird." Lady Bird's mother died when she was five, and she went to live with her Aunt Effie. Lady Bird had few companions besides her aunt and was very shy. But she had no interest in being the "southern belle" her aunt was raising her to become. She forced herself to overcome her shyness by going to journalism school after she graduated from the University of Texas. She became an assertive reporter for the *Daily Texan*.

On their first date, in September 1934, Lyndon took Lady Bird for a car ride. He told her about his work for Kleberg and where he hoped it might lead him. Lady Bird thought their conversation seemed very personal for a first date, particularly when he asked her to marry him. As she later recalled: "I thought it was some kind of joke." She was very intrigued by Lyndon, though. "He was excessively thin, but very, very good-looking, with lots of black wavy hair, and the most outspoken, straightforward, determined manner I had ever encountered."

When Lyndon returned to Washington, he and Lady Bird spoke on the phone and exchanged letters almost daily, and in November they decided to get engaged. Then Lyndon arrived unannounced from Washington, insisting they get married immediately. He took her for another car ride and told her that if she would not marry him that day, she must not love him after all. Lady Bird agreed to marry him immediately, and Lyndon called a friend with influence in the San Antonio City Hall. They got a marriage license that day and were married at St. Mark's Episcopal Church in a simple ceremony attended by a few hastily gathered friends.

Lyndon and Lady Bird rented a house at 1910 Kalorama Road in northwestern Washington. Despite her bashfulness, she frequently entertained Lyndon's fellow secretaries and more important guests, too. Congressman Sam Rayburn was chairman of the Interstate Commerce Committee. Many of the most important New Deal laws regulating business bear his name. "Mr. Sam," as he was called, was a small man with a bald head. But he was powerfully built, and his mouth seemed to be set in a permanent scowl. A kind word or a friendly smile rarely passed his lips.

Claudia "Lady Bird" Taylor was the daughter of an extremely wealthy Texas merchant and landowner. Johnson met her in 1934; on their first date he asked her to marry him.

But Mr. Sam took a shine to young Lyndon and his new bride, joining them regularly for Sunday breakfast and a quiet afternoon reading the papers. Rayburn's face, so stiff and menacing to his colleagues, would light up as he told Lyndon stories about Texas politics. Lyndon listened eagerly, and Mr. Sam was grateful for it. He was a powerful man, but when Congress was not in session, Mr. Sam was often alone. Congressmen were shocked to see the way Rayburn smiled when Lyndon greeted the stern Mr. Sam with a kiss on the top of his bald head.

In June 1935, President Roosevelt announced the creation of the National Youth Administration. NYA offices in each state would offer jobs to unemployed students. The NYA director in Texas had already been sworn in. But after Sam Rayburn visited the White House, it was announced that a mistake had been made and that the director of the NYA in Texas was Lyndon Baines Johnson, the youngest director in the country. Lyndon left Washington, vowing to his friends he would return a congressman.

Lyndon and Lady Bird moved to a rented duplex at 4 Happy Hollow Lane in Austin. Lyndon quickly assembled a staff of 40 young men, many of them former White Stars from San Marcos, and settled into a hectic routine of 12-hour days, 7 days a week. The day started early, and staff members took lunch at their desks. When the electricity was turned off in the building at 10 P.M., they worked by gaslight, and they often adjourned to the back yard of the Johnson home to work late into the night.

Their work paid off. Texas was one of the few states in the country that met its quota of employed students when schools opened in September 1935. By the end of 1936, a total of 20,000 Texans were working under NYA programs. In administering the program's $2 million budget, Lyndon traveled all over the state to start new projects, meeting with prominent figures in Texas politics, including Governor James V. Allred.

In 1937, Austin congressman James P. "Buck" Buchanan died of a heart attack. Lyndon knew this might be his only chance to run for Congress for a long time, and he announced his candidacy. Lyndon's NYA work had made him known to many politicians in the district, but there were nine other candidates, and several had more political experience than Johnson.

However, Lyndon was undaunted. Lady Bird's father gave him $10,000, but money would not be enough. President Roosevelt had recently announced a plan to increase the number of justices on the U.S. Supreme Court. Many people charged the president with trying to increase his powers by "packing" the Court with his own supporters. Several of Lyndon's opponents opposed the plan. Only Lyndon supported it wholeheartedly. Johnson's support for Roosevelt became the center of his campaign.

Lyndon sent his White Stars and NYA men all over the district tacking up posters on trees and fence posts with a single message: A VOTE FOR JOHNSON IS A VOTE FOR ROOSEVELT'S PROGRAM. Lyndon had only 40 days before the election. Although his pro-Roosevelt stand got the support of Governor Allred and Charles Marsh, an important Austin publisher, few voters knew him. He was given little chance of winning.

Lyndon believed the election would be decided in the small towns that politicians rarely visited. Each day he jumped in a car with one or two assistants and crisscrossed the district. Lyndon was awkward delivering a prepared speech, but he was very effective talking to voters one-on-one. He put one hand on their shoulder and held out the other one for a shake, saying, "I hope that you will lend me your helping hand." And as they shook his hand, he would ask where they lived and who they knew there. Soon they were talking warmly about mutual friends.

Frequently he would speak about his work for the NYA. He spoke about the importance of education and about the small part he had played in making sure thousands of young Texans could afford to stay in school. He also spoke about his strong support for Roosevelt's programs to aid farmers.

A poll three days before the election showed the

He made the race in my automobile. . . . He just said he had to have it . . . of course, I turned it over to him. That's the type of fellow he was. He just looked at you, and you belonged to him.
—RAY ROBERTS
a Johnson NYA colleague, on Johnson's campaign for Congress

race to be a toss-up between Lyndon and Assistant Attorney General Merton Harris of Texas. But Lyndon's hard work was taking its toll. He had been living largely on sardines and cheese for several weeks. He had lost 40 pounds. Cramps in his stomach were so painful he could barely stand up. Two days before the election, speaking to the largest crowd of the entire campaign, Lyndon collapsed. He was rushed to a local hospital, and doctors removed his appendix. With Lyndon laid up in a hospital bed, voters in the 10th District went to the polls and made Lyndon Johnson a congressman.

His enthusiastic support for President Roosevelt made headlines in Washington. When FDR visited Texas soon after the election, he invited Lyndon to join him on his whistle-stop tour of Texas. They

Roosevelt is greeted by newly elected Congressman Johnson and Governor James Allred of Texas in 1937. Johnson had made support for Roosevelt one of the most important planks in his congressional campaign platform.

spent the entire day together. Roosevelt offered to help Lyndon get a seat on the Naval Affairs Committee. The president had been assistant secretary of the navy and thought the committee would be a fine place for a young congressman to make a name for himself. Lyndon agreed, and the president gave him the phone number of one of his top aides to call should he need anything.

Apparently, the president was very impressed by Lyndon Johnson. Back in Washington, he told his advisers about "a remarkable young man" he had met in Texas and instructed them to do everything they could to help him. Lyndon Johnson had left Washington vowing to come back a congressman. He had made good on his promise, and he had picked up some very valuable friends along the way.

He was just like a daddy to me always.
—LYNDON JOHNSON on Franklin Roosevelt, after Roosevelt's death

4

Congressman Johnson

Despite Johnson's well-placed friends, he was still only a freshman congressman. The great issues of the day would be immune to his influence. He decided he would be most effective bringing the benefits of the New Deal back to the hill country, and he directed his energies toward clearing the way for a dam to be built at the junction of the Colorado and Pedernales rivers. Congress had already budgeted money for the dam, and a Texas contractor, Herman Brown, had already started building it. Part of the money was for the purchase of the land under the dam by the federal government, but a Texas law made it illegal to sell state land. Only a federal law specifically authorizing the project could save it. Johnson got the law passed in short order.

Herman Brown was a valuable friend for a young politician to have. Brown became one of the wealthiest builders in Texas, thanks in part to federal contracts Johnson helped him secure, and he helped Johnson throughout his career. And because dams can generate electricity, Johnson helped his constituents as well as his own political future by getting the dam built.

I'll tell you this, Lyndon was never anonymous.
—PAUL A. PORTER
FCC Chairman, on Lyndon's early years in Congress

As a young congressman, Johnson was a supporter of President Franklin D. Roosevelt and the New Deal programs he had designed to help the country recover from the Great Depression. Johnson concentrated his efforts on bringing the benefits of the New Deal to his constituents in Texas.

In his first campaign for the Senate, in 1941, Johnson relied on Roosevelt's backing and on his own reputation as a New Deal supporter, but he was defeated by Lee "Pappy" O'Daniel. It was the only election he ever lost.

In America's cities, electricity had lit the streets and powered subways and water pumps for more than a generation. But while the women of urban America did the wash in washing machines, women in the hill country were still filling huge vats with water and scrubbing their clothes with homemade soap, just as Lyndon's mother had when he was a child.

Even with the dam, however, no utility company would run power lines to the small towns in Johnson's district. There were too few customers in the hill country to make it profitable. The same situation held true for many remote, rural areas throughout the United States. Understanding this, President Roosevelt created the Rural Electrification Administration to lend consumers money to form their own utility cooperatives. To qualify for the loan, the Pedernales Electric Cooperative had to sign up at least three families for every square mile.

Johnson's constituents were suspicious of utilities, but Johnson traveled all over the district, trying to convince them to join the co-op. "I believe that river is yours, and the power it can generate belongs to you," he told them. He brought along Sears, Roebuck catalogs to show farmers the washing machines and refrigerators the co-op would allow them to use.

But Johnson's district still did not qualify for the loan, so Johnson went to see President Roosevelt. Before Johnson left Roosevelt's office, FDR got the loan approved. In November 1939, power lines carried electricity to 3,000 hill country families for the first time, and Johnson's constituents knew who they had to thank for it. Parents all over the 10th District began naming their children after Lyndon Johnson.

Johnson's work bringing electricity to the hill country brought him into a circle of young New Dealers. James Rowe, Benjamin Cohen, William O. Douglas, and Tommy "the Cork" Corcoran wrote many of the most important laws of the Roosevelt program. They helped smooth the way for the dam and the co-op loan; in turn, Johnson provided them with information on upcoming votes in Congress. These New Dealers worked together, lived together,

and socialized together, frequently at the Johnsons' home, where Lady Bird was a gracious hostess and Lyndon regaled them with his skills as a Texas storyteller.

Lyndon and Lady Bird also began spending weekends with Charles Marsh, the Austin publisher who had supported Lyndon when he first ran for Congress, and his companion, Alice Glass. Marsh had built a beautiful estate in Virginia for Alice called Longlea. Alice was an idealistic, free-spirited woman. She lived with Marsh for many years but refused to marry him because she did not believe in marriage. Listening to Lyndon's stories about the poverty of the hill country and his plans to improve conditions there, Alice believed Lyndon was more sincere than the other ambitious politicians who visited Longlea. Soon Lyndon was coming to Longlea without Lady Bird, even when Marsh was away. Johnson and Alice Glass became lovers, and their relationship lasted for several years.

Johnson had achieved a great deal for his constituents in his first term, and hill country politicians knew it would be futile to challenge him. He ran unopposed in the 1940 election.

Still, he was very active in the campaign. The Democrats were concentrating all their resources on defeating President Roosevelt's Republican opponent, Wendell Willkie. Because of this, the party had little money to help congressional candidates, and

An excited Johnson and jubilant campaign workers celebrate his lead in the Texas senatorial race. The celebration, however, was premature—he lost by 1,311 votes.

polls showed the Democrats could lose 60 seats in the House.

With just three weeks before the election, Johnson asked Herman Brown and Charles Marsh to raise as much money as they could immediately. When he notified candidates that he had secured funds for them, he also sent them questionnaires about how well the president was running in their district. The candidates were seasoned political observers, and Johnson passed along their information to the president's advisers. He also analyzed each congressional race himself and found the Democrats could lose 80 seats, 20 more than the party expected. FDR was impressed by Johnson. The Democrats fared much better than anyone believed possible. Far from the big losses they expected, they actually gained eight seats.

Congress reconvened in 1941, and the same name, Lyndon Johnson, kept turning up when congressmen compared notes about their campaigns. After only one term, Johnson had broken out of the pack of junior congressmen. The word went out on Capitol Hill that he was a congressman worth getting to know.

Despite his success, Johnson would later say his first few years in Congress left him "terribly restless and unhappy." Most likely this was because he knew it would take years for the seniority system to deliver him to higher responsibilities in the House leadership.

When U.S. senator Morris Sheppard of Texas died on April 9, 1941, Johnson saw a way out of his dilemma. He would run for Sheppard's Senate seat. Thanks to Herman Brown and Charles Marsh, Johnson no longer had any trouble raising money. His main problem was that he was unknown to most voters outside his own district. Early polls showed him far behind Attorney General Gerald C. Mann, of Texas, a populist who had clamped down on violations of antitrust laws by the big interests.

Johnson focused his campaign on his support for FDR, but that was about the only similarity between this campaign and his 1937 House race. For one thing, Johnson was running for statewide office, and Texas was too big for Johnson to visit each of its small towns and meet voters one by one, as he had done in 1937. Instead he blanketed the state with radio ads. Johnson's manner and appearance also changed. His gaunt cheeks had filled out to reveal a double chin. He wore dark blue suits with a carnation in the lapel, and glasses in which he read his long speeches in a formal, "senatorial" tone.

His new style paid off. Within a few weeks he was trailing Mann by only a few points. But then Governor W. Lee "Pappy" O'Daniel entered the race. Before he became governor, Pappy had been the most popular radio personality in the state. His songs about motherhood, cowboys, and religious faith tugged at the heartstrings of Texas. As governor, however, he had so alienated the legislature that the state government had ground to a halt. But he was still popular with the voters.

> *I don't know what they did, but whatever it was, apparently it was effective.*
> —JAMES BLUNDELL
> Johnson's aide, on W. Lee O'Daniel's victory over Johnson in senate race

49

Johnson became very depressed after Pappy entered the race. He lost his voice and came down with pneumonia. After two weeks in the hospital, however, he returned to the campaign with a new fire, turning his campaign into an "All-Out Patriotic Revue" complete with singers, comedians, bands, and a lottery drawing. Bowing to O'Daniel's popularity, Johnson told the voters that Pappy was such a good governor they should keep him in Texas. Pappy had pledged to stay in Austin until the legislature approved the state budget, and he did not get to respond to Johnson's charge until the last week of the campaign.

With nearly all the votes counted on the night of the election, Johnson was leading O'Daniel by 13,000 votes. The news was so good that Johnson's supporters carried him on their shoulders through the Stephen F. Austin Hotel, where he awaited the final returns. It seemed that only a miracle could defeat him.

The stricken USS _West Virginia_ blazes in the aftermath of the bombing of the U.S. naval base at Pearl Harbor in December 1941, while a small boat rescues a seaman from the water. The American response to the attack was an immediate declaration of war on Japan.

Over the next few days, a miracle did defeat him. As votes from rural districts trickled in, Johnson's lead shrank to 77 votes. The next day, "corrected" vote totals began coming in, and before it was over, Johnson had lost by just 1,311 votes. Many people believed Pappy's supporters had cheated Johnson out of the election. President Roosevelt teased him that "apparently you Texans haven't learned one of the first things we learned up in New York State, and that is that when the election is over, you have to sit on the ballot boxes."

On December 7, 1941, the Japanese bombed Pearl Harbor. Lyndon Johnson was the first member of Congress to volunteer for service in World War II. He was stationed in San Francisco, where he trained naval employees in war production work.

In the spring of 1942, President Roosevelt appointed Johnson to inspect military installations in General Douglas MacArthur's command in the Southwest Pacific. Johnson was made a lieutenant commander in the navy. The Japanese had driven MacArthur out of the Philippines, and he had established headquarters in Australia. Johnson and two other officers arrived in Australia on May 25, 1942. MacArthur had ordered a bombing run over Japanese-held territory in New Guinea, and Johnson asked to go along. Several planes had been lost on similar missions, and MacArthur was not anxious to lose a congressman. But Johnson insisted he had come "to see personally for the president just what conditions are like, and I cannot find out what they are like if I don't go along."

As the American planes approached their target, the Japanese were waiting for them. One plane was shot down, and Johnson's plane lost power five minutes from the target. The plane dropped its bombs and turned back, pursued by eight Japanese Zeros. One crewman later recalled that, as the Japanese pelted the plane, Johnson was "just as calm as if we were on a sight-seeing tour." The plane was so badly damaged that the crew made an emergency landing. MacArthur awarded Johnson a Silver Star, the third highest decoration for valor awarded by the U.S. Army.

During World War II, Johnson served as a lieutenant commander in the navy. He was the first member of Congress to volunteer for service.

Shortly after, Roosevelt issued a directive instructing congressmen in the military to return to Washington and resume their legislative duties. Johnson gave several speeches on the House floor as an expert on the war effort, and he was reelected in 1942 without opposition. Johnson would later say that World War II had had a decisive influence on his foreign-policy views. "I learned that war comes about by two things — by a lust for power on the part of a few evil leaders and by a weakness on the part of the people whose love for peace too often displays a lack of courage that serves as an open invitation to all the aggressors of the world." This belief that nations sometimes have to fight wars to preserve peace would animate his conduct of the Vietnam War when he became president 20 years later.

Having seen his father reduced to poverty in middle age, Johnson worried that the same thing could happen to him. He knew that being a congressman was no guarantee of financial security; Johnson had once met a Capitol Hill elevator operator who informed him that he, too, had once been a congressman. In 1942, the Johnsons began to accumulate the wealth that would make them the wealthiest first family ever to enter the White House.

They bought KTBC, an Austin radio station. Although Johnson always insisted that Lady Bird ran the station, biographers have found that Johnson was active in the business, soliciting advertisers and acquiring a lucrative affiliation with the Columbia Broadcasting System (CBS). By 1951, the Johnsons' Texas Broadcasting Corporation was earning annual profits of nearly $60,000. KTBC became a television station, and the Federal Communications Commission turned down all other requests for television broadcasting licenses in Austin, giving KTBC a monopoly. Many writers have suggested that the FCC gave the Johnsons special treatment, but no one has ever shown that Johnson asked the FCC for favors. By 1963, when Johnson became president, the Johnsons owned several broadcasting properties worth a total of $7 million and had put their annual profits of $500,000 into extensive holdings in real estate and bank stock.

As the Johnsons began to secure their future, they also started a family to share it with. Lynda Bird was born in 1944, and their second daughter, Luci Baines, was born a year later. It was characteristic of Johnson that his entire family shared his initials, LBJ. He was a demanding husband, expecting Lady Bird to manage their household, entertain his friends, and assume all the public duties of a politician's wife. Lady Bird's shyness made these expectations difficult to meet in their early years together. But by the 1940s she had grown more comfortable with public life. She had even run Lyndon's congressional office during the war. Lyndon depended a great deal on her affection and support and often said she was the only person whose loyalty and judgment he could truly trust. The birth of their children brought them still closer together.

The liberal years of the New Deal ended with World War II. The poverty and economic depression of the 1930s had ended, but America was haunted by the specter of communism at home and abroad during

Johnson and Lady Bird with daughters Lynda Bird (left), born in 1944, and Luci Baines, born a year later. The photo was taken in August 1948, as Johnson awaited the runoff that would result in his election to the U.S. Senate.

Inside the image: COMMUNIST PARTY ORGANIZATION U.S.A-FEB 9,1950

Senator Joseph McCarthy of Wisconsin (with pointer) conducted an irresponsible campaign, characterized by baseless accusations and innuendo against alleged communists, in the government. His success reflected the surge of anticommunist sentiment in the United States in the wake of World War II.

the postwar years. During the war, the Soviet Union and the United States had been allies against Germany and Japan, but after the war, that friendship gave way to conflict and suspicion when the United States refused to surrender its monopoly on atomic weapons and the Soviet Union installed communist governments in several Eastern European countries. Thus the prolabor policies of the New Deal were replaced by a conservative, probusiness climate as much of the public became suspicious of the demands and political loyalties of workers.

Johnson's liberal populism showed a new emphasis on national unity after the war. He still opposed the big interests. But he now believed the federal government needed to keep both unions and corporations in check. He supported a law that would have undermined the right to strike, a keystone of New Deal liberalism. And he took a hard line against the Soviet Union.

In 1948, Johnson ran for the U.S. Senate again. The campaign reflected the new conservative climate in the United States; the main issues were the power of unions and the threat of communism. Johnson's main opponent in the Democratic primary, former Texas governor Coke R. Stevenson, was an anti–New Dealer who opposed unions and military spending. He accused Johnson of voting with communist sympathizers in Congress. Johnson charged that Stevenson's opposition to military spending would invite the Soviet Union to start a war the same way conservatives had encouraged Hitler's aggression by opposing a military buildup before World War II.

Running on a platform of "peace, prosperity, and progress," Johnson traveled the state by helicopter. Few Texans had ever seen a helicopter before, and when the "Johnson City Windmill" touched down in pastures and baseball fields, people came from miles around to see the candidate. Johnson's helicopter touched down 20 times a day, and he lost 27 pounds in the furious campaign. The night before the election Lady Bird cut up a telephone book and divided it up among her mother-in-law and two sisters. They called every voter they could, asking them to vote for Lyndon. There were nine candidates in the election, and Johnson did well enough to force a runoff with Stevenson.

Johnson was worried that he might lose the runoff. He had given up his seat in the House to run for the Senate; if he lost the election, he would be out of politics entirely. Exhausted by the pace of the election, Johnson was hospitalized with kidney stones three weeks before the runoff. But when he returned to the campaign, he secured endorsements from union leaders who would get the vote out. Stevenson narrowly led Johnson when the ballots were counted on election day. But as the returns came in from the rural districts, Johnson caught up. By the end of the counting, Johnson had won by just 87 votes out of 900,000 ballots cast. Stevenson charged that Johnson had stuffed the ballot boxes, just as Pappy O'Daniel had been rumored to do in 1941, and took his challenge all the way to the U.S. Supreme Court, but the Court declared the matter out of its jurisdiction. Johnson then easily defeated his Republican opponent in the general election.

In 1939, Johnson had returned to Washington as a congressman. Now, in 1949, he was moving up to the Senate. The coming years would take him higher still.

5

Master of the Senate

Lyndon Johnson's rise to the Senate brought him again to the bottom of the heap. A coalition of Republicans and conservative southern Democrats chaired all the major committees. This "inner club," as it was called, decided which legislation the full Senate voted on and held the balance of power that determined which side won those votes.

Johnson concentrated his efforts on keeping in touch with his constituents. He expected his staff to handle 650 letters, 500 phone calls, and 70 visitors each day. As a legislator, Johnson decided he would have the most impact if he specialized in one area. He became an expert on national defense issues and got a seat on the Armed Services Committee, which oversaw the nation's military budget.

The inner club and the seniority system made the Senate a stifling place for most of its young members. First-term senators such as Johnson were expected to be seen and not heard. But the Senate was tailor-made for Johnson's skills at personal persuasion. This ability had allowed him to control the White Stars and the Little Congress, elevating his status at San Marcos and on Capitol Hill in a very short time. Johnson realized that if he could gain the trust of the inner club, he could rise out of the pack of junior senators.

Mr. Johnson took to the Senate as if he'd been born there. From the first day on it was obvious that it was his place . . . just the right size.
—WALTER JENKINS
Johnson aide

Johnson relaxes with his dog, Beagle, at the LBJ Ranch in 1956. Johnson's grasp of the legislative process and his instincts for negotiation and compromise made him a very effective senator.

Rebekah Baines Johnson congratulates her son upon his election to a second term as a U.S. senator. In his hands are telegrams from well-wishers.

Senator Richard Russell, a conservative Democrat from Georgia, was chairman of the Armed Services Committee and the leader of the inner club. Johnson, as a member of his committee, worked with Russell on a daily basis. Russell believed strongly in the gentility of the Old South. And Johnson showered Russell with a charm and politeness he had never before displayed.

Johnson developed a strong respect for Russell's devotion to the Senate. Russell's entire life revolved around it. He arrived on Capitol Hill early enough to have breakfast there and stayed well into the evenings, usually eating a late dinner nearby. Frequently the only senator Russell would see on the Hill at those early and late hours was Lyndon Johnson, and they dined together often. Capitol Hill was deserted on Sundays, so on many occasions Johnson invited Russell over for breakfast and a quiet afternoon reading the papers, just as he had often spent his Sundays with Sam Rayburn a decade before. "He [Russell] was my mentor and I wanted to take care of him," Johnson later said.

Russell and the other southern Democrats of the inner club were strict segregationists. Although Johnson would later, as president, take a strong stand on civil rights, in 1950 he voted with the segregationists to oppose bills against lynchings and poll taxes (taxes imposed as a prerequisite for voting), which prevented many southern blacks from voting. He later said he opposed these bills because "at that time I simply did not believe that the legislation, as written, was the right way to handle the problem. Much of it seemed designed more to humiliate the South than to help the black man."

Johnson also became more adamantly nonideological in his political views during his first years in the Senate. He described himself as a "a liberal, a conservative, a Texan, a taxpayer, a rancher, a businessman, a consumer, a parent, a voter, and not as young as I used to be nor as old as I expect to be—and I am all these things in no fixed order."

Johnson and Lady Bird wave farewell in August 1955, as they depart Washington for Texas, where the senator would recuperate from his heart attack. The strain of being Senate majority leader had taken a toll on Johnson's health.

The members of the inner club were so powerful they did not even bother controlling the party leadership positions that members of the House waited decades to assume. But just as Johnson had seen the political potential of the White Stars and the Little Congress, so he recognized that the offices of the Senate leadership could play an important role in that body. In 1950 the position of Democratic party whip, the number-two position among Senate Democrats, became available, and Johnson asked Russell for his support. At the age of 42, Johnson was elected the youngest party whip in history. In 1953, Johnson became Senate minority leader, the top position among Senate Democrats. And when the Democrats obtained a majority in the Senate in 1955, Johnson became majority leader.

But Johnson was majority leader of the Senate in name only. The inner club still controlled the major committees and thereby controlled the Senate as a whole. So Johnson set about establishing a more prominent role for the majority leader's office.

Johnson tried to loosen the inner club's hold over the Senate by opening up the seniority system. He developed a proposal to guarantee each senator a seat on at least one important committee, regardless of how many terms the senator had served. But Johnson knew the Senate would not adopt the proposal without the inner club's support, and many members of the inner club were likely to see the proposal as a threat to their power. Johnson told Russell that the Senate was filled with talented young men whose energy and intelligence were being wasted because they were excluded from the best committees. The proposal appealed to Russell's commitment to the Senate as an institution, and he convinced the rest of the inner club to accept it. As majority leader, Johnson helped decide which Democratic senators were assigned to the important committees, and younger Democratic senators recognized Johnson as their champion.

The majority leader automatically became chairman of the Democratic Policy Committee. The committee was supposed to plan legislative strategy for the Democrats, but it rarely did more than follow the lead of the inner club. Johnson transformed the committee into a forum through which Democrats decided what bills the Senate would vote on. Any senator who wanted to expedite or delay a bill now needed Johnson's help in doing so.

On the floor of the Senate, Johnson seemed to be in constant motion, gathering votes, brokering compromises, controlling everything from the length of debates to the pace of the roll call. Johnson established a rule that committed the leadership of both parties to reach, whenever possible, unanimous agreements limiting debate to a specified amount of time for each side. He developed hand signals with Senate clerks. If a vote was going well, Johnson would twirl his index finger in the air, and the vote would go quickly. If he was waiting for a senator whose vote he was counting on, he would push the palm of his hand down, and the roll call would proceed slowly.

Many historians believe Johnson was the most powerful majority leader the Senate ever had. The "Johnson treatment" became a Washington legend. When Johnson needed a senator's vote, he would bend his six-foot, three-inch frame down into the face of his colleague and put one arm around his shoulder, just as his father had in Austin. When the target of his persuasion resisted, Johnson's arm would slip down to the lapel of his colleague's jacket, and his cajoling praise would turn into intense rebuke.

The effort Johnson put into running the Senate took its toll. By the summer of 1955 he was constantly tired. He agreed to take a break over the Fourth of July weekend only at Lady Bird's insistence. But when he arrived at Herman Brown's estate in Middleburg, Virginia, he complained that he was short of breath and felt faint. Johnson refused to have a doctor called until another guest, Senator Clinton Anderson, warned Johnson that he might be having a heart attack. Anderson was right. Johnson was indeed having a heart attack, and he spent four months recovering from it. Lady Bird and Johnson's mother helped him recuperate at the LBJ Ranch near Johnson City, which he and Lady Bird

He was a very good majority leader. He worked the Senate. If he had a job to do, we didn't go home at five or six o'clock. We went home when we got the job done, and it might be two or three days later.
—BARRY GOLDWATER
Republican senator
from Arizona

had bought in 1948. Not surprisingly, Johnson found his inactivity difficult. His moods swung rapidly between anger and enthusiasm One moment he was talking about resigning, and the next he was bursting into activity.

Johnson returned to the Senate fully recovered on January 2, 1956. The civil rights issue had been simmering for decades, and now it was coming to a head. After the Civil War, southern states began to pass segregation laws separating blacks and whites in their daily lives. These "Jim Crow" laws gave the force of law to the Whites Only signs that greeted blacks at public water fountains, rest rooms, restaurants, hotels, movie theaters — any place where whites chose to exclude blacks. In 1896, the U.S. Supreme Court's decision in the case of *Plessy v. Ferguson* endorsed the legality of Jim Crow laws. The Court declared that "separate but equal" facilities in train stations and railroad cars did not violate the Constitution. The decision reassured southern states that the federal government would not oppose segregation. Jim Crow laws became increasingly strict.

Racial segregation was the law of the land in the South in the 1950s. Johnson's pragmatic approach to the Civil Rights Act of 1957 — he agreed to water down the bill after objections from southern senators threatened to delay legislation — earned him much criticism.

FOR COLORED ONLY

In the 1930s segregation came under increasing criticism throughout the country. Liberals, Socialists, and Communists began to give legal aid to the victims of southern racism. After World War II, the federal government began to remove its *imprimatur* from segregationist practices. In 1948, President Truman ordered the gradual desegregation of the armed forces. In 1954 the Supreme Court declared in its momentous *Brown v. Board of Education* decision that segregation by race in public schools was unconstitutional.

In the fall of 1956 white mobs in Tennessee and Texas tried to prevent blacks from entering white schools. The governors of Texas and Arkansas refused to enforce the Supreme Court's desegregation ruling. Pressure mounted for federal legislation on civil rights. President Dwight D. Eisenhower submitted legislation to create a Civil Rights Division in the federal Justice Department and a Civil Rights Commission to recommend further legislative remedies for discrimination. The bill also proposed authorizing the Justice Department to file suits against southerners who prevented blacks from exercising their right to vote. But Congress rejected the measure.

In May 1954, the U.S. Supreme Court ruled that segregation in public schools was unconstitutional. The Court's decision met with delay and outright defiance in the South.

President Dwight D. Eisenhower in 1954. A great supporter of Johnson, he was one of the first to predict that the Texas senator would someday become president.

In the following year, however, Johnson assembled a coalition that passed the Civil Rights Act of 1957, the first civil rights legislation approved by the Senate in 87 years. Johnson was determined that civil rights legislation proposed by a Republican administration not be defeated a second time by a Senate under Democratic control. Johnson convinced Russell that if the South refused to compromise, liberals would simply propose an even stronger measure and eventually would have their way. Johnson promised to remove a provision of the bill authorizing the federal government to send agents into the states to protect civil rights. The South considered this provision an intrusion of the federal government into the affairs of state governments. With this provision removed, Russell and other southerners reluctantly agreed to support the bill.

Liberals criticized Johnson's compromise for diluting the bill. They did not believe the Eisenhower administration would use its new authority to initiate suits on behalf of blacks whose voting rights had been violated. But without Johnson's compromise, the South would have defeated the bill's other provisions creating the Civil Rights Commission and a Civil Rights Division in the Justice Department. Johnson's compromise also prevented a major split in the Democratic party between southern conservatives and northern liberals.

In 1958 Johnson headed a committee that drafted the first legislation on American space exploration. The Soviet Union had just sent the first artificial satellite, *Sputnik I*, into space. Many people feared that the United States would fall behind the Soviets in the military applications of space exploration. In fact, there was considerable pressure to give control of the space program entirely to the military. Johnson's legislation struck a compromise by allowing the Pentagon to oversee military space projects but leaving the peaceful exploration of space entirely in civilian hands. The Space Act of 1958 created the National Aeronautics and Space Administration, which still presides over civilian space exploration.

Johnson's critics charged that he increased the power of the majority leader in the Senate but diminished the influence of the Senate as a whole. By cooperating with President Eisenhower and restricting debate in the Senate, Johnson failed to offer the country an alternative to the Republicans' conservative policies.

But Johnson was above all a pragmatist. He had no interest in fighting battles over principle if they would be losing battles. He believed the country was firmly behind Eisenhower and later said that he chose to work with him to maintain national unity. "The biggest danger to American stability is the politics of principle, which brings out the masses in irrational fights for unlimited goals. . . . It is for nothing else than the sake of national stability that I consider myself a consensus man," he said. Johnson felt particularly strongly that the Senate should support the president on foreign-policy matters. "If you're in an airplane and you're flying somewhere, you don't run to the cockpit and attack the pilot. Mr. Eisenhower is the only president we've got."

Eisenhower appreciated Johnson's cooperative attitude. In late 1958 he welcomed Johnson to a meeting of legislative leaders in the Cabinet Room of the White House. Motioning toward the high-backed chair the president usually sat in, Eisenhower said to Johnson, "You sit there."

"Oh, no," Johnson replied. "That's your chair, Mr. President."

"It'll be yours someday," Eisenhower said with a grin.

"No," Johnson replied. "I will never sit in that chair."

But by 1959, many people began to think that Eisenhower was right. In October, Johnson's supporters in Texas, led by Sam Rayburn, announced that they had formed a Johnson for President Committee. Over the next six months, Texas politicians fanned out across the South and Far West with the message "All the way with LBJ."

But Johnson was ambivalent. He wanted to be president, but he was unsure of himself as a na-

If I ever got the power, I said I'm going to do something about it, and now I've got the power, and I am going to do something.
—LYNDON JOHNSON
on his vow to
fight prejudice

tional leader. Although he had been one of the most powerful politicians in the country, he believed a southerner would never be accepted by the members of the "establishment" in the Northeast, who would play a key role in selecting the Democratic nominee for president. But Johnson and his supporters also believed that no candidate would emerge from the primaries with enough votes to win the nomination. After several years in the Senate and House leadership, Johnson and Rayburn believed they would be in an excellent position to swing votes to Johnson at a deadlocked convention.

Johnson believed his Senate colleagues would control their state delegations at the Democratic convention in Los Angeles. So Johnson spent most of the campaign in Washington, seeking the support of his fellow senators. In the 1952 or 1956 elections, Johnson's strategy might very well have worked. But by 1960, the most important figures in the Democratic party were no longer senators but governors and state party chairmen. And as John F. Kennedy, a youthful senator from Massachusetts, crisscrossed the country, he obtained their support. Only in the last few weeks of the primary campaign did Johnson travel extensively around the country, but by then it was already too late. Kennedy won the nomination on the first ballot at the convention.

Speaker of the House Sam Rayburn, a fellow Texan, receives a kiss on the head from Johnson during a party in honor of Rayburn's 76th birthday. Rayburn was one of Johnson's first and most powerful mentors in Washington, and he spearheaded Johnson's 1960 presidential campaign.

The campaign between Johnson and Kennedy had been hard fought, and neither candidate thought the other had fought a completely fair fight. But the end of the campaign rekindled the mutual respect between the two candidates. There was talk that Kennedy would ask Johnson to be his vice-president. Many of Johnson's supporters warned him that he would find the largely ceremonial duties of the vice-presidency unfulfilling compared to the hurly-burly of running the Senate. But Lady Bird thought the job of majority leader had been too strenuous for any man, particularly one with a history of heart problems. She welcomed the slower pace of the vice-presidency. Johnson believed he could make the vice-presidency an important position, just as he had transformed the White Stars, the Little Congress, and the majority leader's office into powerful institutions. When Kennedy offered Johnson the vice-presidency, Johnson accepted.

An enthusiastic Johnson backer shows her support for the candidate in 1960, but it was John Kennedy who won the Democratic party's nomination for president.

6

The Presidency

Johnson hoped his experience on Capitol Hill would allow him to help President Kennedy implement his programs. Senator Mike Mansfield, Johnson's successor as majority leader, asked the Democrats to allow Johnson to preside over meetings of the Democratic caucus. Many senators had resented the control Johnson had exerted over them as majority leader, and they were not eager to place themselves under his authority now that he was in the White House. Johnson's former Senate colleagues rejected the proposal. Johnson, hurt by the decision, retreated from any involvement with the Senate.

Johnson chafed under the burden of his ceremonial duties as vice-president. For 30 years he had been a whirlwind of activity, never far from the center of power and action in Washington. Now he spent most of his time meeting visiting dignitaries and substituting for the president at funerals and other state functions for which Johnson had little patience.

I have worked beside more than three thousand members of Congress from every nook and cranny of America. Every great leader of this past century I have known personally. I think I know a great leader when I see him.
—SAM RAYBURN
Democratic Speaker of the House, from his speech to nominate Johnson for president

Kennedy and Johnson worked well together in the White House, but Johnson felt frustrated by his role as vice-president. Though Johnson was in many ways more active than previous vice-presidents, he was dissatisfied with being only second in command.

Nonetheless, Johnson did play a more active role than most vice-presidents. He was chairman of the President's Committee on Equal Employment Opportunity and chairman of the Space Council. He also traveled widely, visiting 33 countries on 11 goodwill tours and fact-finding missions. During these trips Johnson seemed like his old flamboyant and energetic self. For instance, while in India's famous Taj Mahal he let out a loud Texas whoop to test the structure's echo. Official Washington found Johnson's behavior boorish, but he felt a strong bond with the people he met abroad, particularly with the poor people of Third World nations. Walking through the slums of New Delhi, Johnson passed out gifts by the dozen, shaking hands, patting heads, meeting and greeting the public as if he were campaigning for reelection in the Texas hill country.

By 1963, Kennedy and Johnson were campaigning for reelection. But their campaign together ended in Johnson's native Texas almost before it had begun. Two shots from Lee Harvey Oswald's rifle ended the Kennedy presidency in a tragedy that shocked the world. President Johnson later recalled that during his flight from Dallas to Washington on *Air Force One*, "I made a solemn private vow: I would devote every hour of every day during the remainder of John Kennedy's unfulfilled term to achieving the goals he had set."

Kennedy's forceful presence had been felt during his 34 months in the White House. His wit and eloquence challenged the nation to eradicate poverty and to explore the new frontier in space. He had brought the nation back from the brink of nuclear war during the Cuban missile crisis, and he had signed a treaty with the Soviet Union banning above-ground tests of nuclear weapons. Congress left most of his domestic agenda unfulfilled, however. But with his death, the American people forgot what he had left undone and remembered his ringing calls to action, his youthful sophistication, and the hope he had instilled in them.

In contrast to the cool, principled statesman the nation saw in President John F. Kennedy, Lyndon

B. Johnson seemed like a swaggering, back-room wheeler-dealer. Clearly, Majority Leader Johnson was a skilled politician. But Americans wondered whether President Johnson could lead the nation out of its grief and on to the challenges that lay ahead.

On November 27, five days after Kennedy's assassination, President Johnson mounted the rostrum of the House. Under the glare of television lights, he spoke to the nation in soft and subdued tones that conveyed a deep sense of humility. He called on the country to put aside its divisions and honor President Kennedy by supporting his programs. "Let us put an end to the teaching and the preaching of hate and evil and violence," he said. "Let us turn away from the fanatics of the Far Left and the Far Right, from the apostles of bitterness and bigotry, from those defiant of law and those who pour venom into our nation's bloodstream." By the end of the speech, the assembled congressmen, Supreme Court justices, and foreign dignitaries were on their feet, applauding the memory of President Kennedy and the leadership of President Johnson.

Johnson's remarkable energy, dormant during his years as vice-president, redoubled when he be-

Kennedy speaks to the press on the Vietnam issue. He increased the U.S. military presence in Vietnam, a policy that Johnson was to continue.

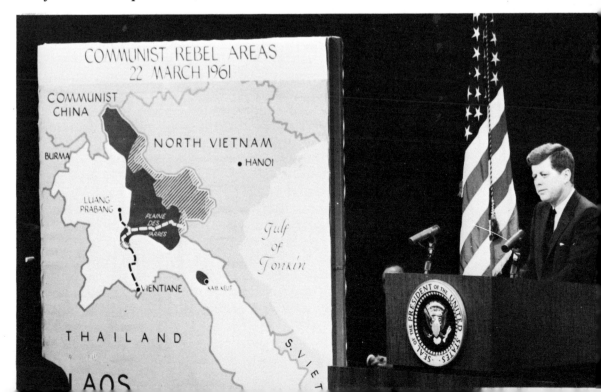

came president. He began a routine he called the "two-shift day," beginning with a review of the day's schedule while he was still in his bedroom at 6:30 A.M. At 2:00 P.M. he left the Oval Office for a walk or a swim before lunch and then a nap. At 4:00 P.M., he showered and changed for the second shift, which rarely ended before 2:00 A.M. the next morning.

No task was too small to command Johnson's attention. He seemed to have his hands in everything that went on at the White House — even reviewing the guest list at state dinners. He had telephones installed all over the White House — in the dining room, movie theater, his sitting room, and bathroom — to make sure he was never more than a few feet away from his work. He even had a special floating telephone for the White House pool.

On the other end of all those phones was a troop of loyal aides. When Johnson wanted something, he usually wanted it immediately. He harried his staff with an unpredictable cascade of praise and fury. Johnson's aides could be identified by their stride, usually something between a trot and a dead run. Indeed, the Johnson staff seemed to be in perpetual motion, just like the president they served.

Having worked on Capitol Hill for more than 30 years, Johnson knew how to gauge the mood of Congress. He knew the key players and how to appeal to them. He liked to tell congressmen that "our house is your house," and he proved it with frequent invitations to the White House. Johnson socialized with congressmen in part because he liked nothing better than an evening discussing politics. But he also knew congressmen appreciated an intimate evening with the president. It made them feel important. And it established a personal rapport with individual legislators that would be helpful when Johnson needed their support.

And when Johnson needed a congressman's help, the congressman received casual phone calls from the president. Johnson would compliment him on a recent speech. He told him how much he valued the congressman's advice. Often he would offer his help. Perhaps the congressman would join him for a walk around the White House, where photographers were sure to get a picture? Was the congressman's district receiving its fair share of federally funded construction projects? And, when all else failed, there was always the famous Johnson treatment.

With the country's affection for President Kennedy at its height, Johnson applied his gift for personal persuasion to enacting Kennedy's unfinished agenda. Civil rights legislation and a tax cut had both gained strong support in the House before Kennedy's death, so Johnson made passing these bills in the Senate his highest priority.

Johnson moved first on a tax reduction. Senator Harry F. Byrd was chairman of the committee that would decide whether the Senate would vote on the Tax Reduction Act of 1964. But Senator Byrd thought the government was already spending too much money. A tax cut would only make a bad situation worse. Johnson ordered every government agency to cut its budget. And before announcing the results, Johnson invited Byrd over to the White House for a drink and a private look at the budget. Johnson explained that he had cut $500 million from the budget, and he persuaded Byrd that he was serious about lowering government spending. Byrd agreed to submit the tax cut for a vote by the full Senate. Several senators tried to add tax breaks for their particular supporters, everyone from oil men to ballpoint pen manufacturers. But Johnson bombarded the Senate with phone calls to make sure the bill passed without these additions. The bill had languished in Congress for 13 months under President Kennedy. President Johnson got it passed in just 96 days.

Johnson moved next on civil rights. In the summer of 1963, 200,000 Americans, black and white, demonstrated in Washington in favor of federal civil rights legislation. The civil rights movement was gaining strength, spreading its commitment to bring segregation to an end.

Senator Richard B. Russell believed that if he could delay the bill long enough, Johnson would withdraw it to avoid splitting the Democratic party

> *Johnson had a gut commitment for changing the entire social fabric of this country. . . . I don't think we would ever have got the civil rights legislation we did without Johnson.*
> —ROBERT C. WEAVER
> president, Baruch College

at the upcoming 1964 convention. But Johnson was determined not to preside over another compromise, as he had in 1957. Instead, he stood his ground against his old friend. He told Russell he would stand by the bill even if it bottled up the Senate for months. Furthermore, he declared that if the bill did not pass by July, he would call Congress back into session after the convention.

But Johnson realized he still did not have enough votes to pass the bill without Republican support. And Republicans would not support a Democratic president in an election year unless Minority Leader Everett McKinley Dirksen, the top Republican in the Senate, told them to do so. Johnson knew that Dirksen liked to put a Republican stamp on major legislation, so he encouraged Dirksen to submit whatever changes in the bill he thought would gain Republican support for it — as long as the White House could approve the changes first. Thus Johnson won Republican support by apparently giving Dirksen control over the bill without ever committing himself to changes he would oppose.

On July 2, a beaming President Johnson, with Dirksen and several civil rights leaders at his side, signed the Civil Rights Act of 1964. The law prohibited discrimination against blacks in public accommodations. Jim Crow laws could no longer exclude blacks from hotels, movie theaters, or any other public establishment. The law also required every hospital, school, and college that received money from the federal government — 35,000 institutions in all 50 states — to end discriminatory practices.

Johnson had won congressional approval for two key elements of the Kennedy program. In May he put his own stamp on the presidency in a speech at the University of Michigan. Johnson believed America stood at the threshold of a new era in its history. From the founding of the Republic until the 1870s, Americans had moved west, laying claim to a land rich with natural resources. From the 1870s through World War II and the postwar era, Americans had used those national resources to make themselves the wealthiest people the world have ever known.

Now, Johnson argued the United States faced a new challenge. "The challenge of the next half-century is whether we have the wisdom to use that wealth to enrich and elevate our national life. . . . For in our time we have the opportunity to move not only toward the rich society and powerful society, but upward to the Great Society."

Johnson had shown he could lead the nation out of the tragedy of President Kennedy's death. With this speech, he offered the nation his vision of the challenges that lay ahead.

The nation responded. Polls showed that nearly three quarters of all Americans approved of Johnson's performance as president. Journalists described Lyndon Johnson as "a healer," his presidency as "a miracle."

When it came time for the Democratic party to nominate a candidate for the 1964 presidential election, Johnson's support at the Democratic National Convention in Atlantic City was so strong that the only question was whom he would select as his running mate for vice-president. In order to create some suspense about the choice, Johnson asked Senator

Eager admirers reach out for a handshake with Johnson in Scranton, Pennsylvania in 1964. That year Johnson was reelected president in an unprecedented landslide.

Hubert H. Humphrey of Minnesota and Senator
Thomas J. Dodd of Connecticut to fly to the convention together, even though Johnson had already
decided on Humphrey.

On July 15, the Republicans chose Senator Barry
Goldwater of Arizona as their presidential nominee.
Watching the convention on television, Johnson
smiled broadly as Goldwater walked to the podium
to accept the nomination. Johnson had a poll in his
pocket showing that Americans favored him over
Goldwater by more than two to one.

After eight years of moderate Republicanism under Eisenhower, Goldwater's nomination marked a
return to a more extreme conservatism that Americans had not seen since they turned Herbert Hoover
out of office over 30 years earlier. Goldwater's
tanned good looks and flamboyant statements gave
his seemingly outdated views a new look. But many
Americans were frightened by Goldwater's rash
statements about nuclear weapons. "I want to lob
one into the men's room of the Kremlin and make
sure I hit it," he said with a grin. Goldwater also
said he would use nuclear weapons in Vietnam, fo-
cusing public attention for the first time on America's long involvement in the war there.

Under President Truman the United States had

provided military aid to France, whose status as a colonial ruler in Vietnam was being increasingly threatened by a nationalist movement of communist rebels led by Ho Chi Minh. Ho and his forces defeated the French in a decisive battle in 1954. The French withdrew, and Vietnam was temporarily divided into two countries. A communist government ruled North Vietnam, and a pro-Western government ruled South Vietnam. Eisenhower committed the United States to sending economic and military aid to South Vietnam.

Eisenhower hoped that American aid would allow South Vietnam to institute social reforms that would make communism less popular and to build up its military forces to keep the North Vietnamese at bay. President Kennedy continued this policy, but he sharply increased the number of American military advisers to 17,000. Nonetheless, the South

Missouri campaign workers tack up posters for Johnson and Goldwater in 1964. The Republican's selection of Goldwater as their presidential candidate marked the party's return to conservatism, but Johnson won an overwhelming victory in November.

Ho Chi Minh led the successful Vietnamese struggle against French colonial rule. As the president of North Vietnam until 1969, he presided over the war that pitted his country and its Vietcong (communist guerrilla) allies against South Vietnam and the United States.

Vietnamese government, divided and corrupt, continued to lose support. Economic reform was slow in coming, and South Vietnamese nationalists resented the government's dependence on the United States. At the same time, the Communists in South Vietnam, known as the Vietcong, continued to grow in strength. The Vietcong, aided by North Vietnam, sought to overthrow the South Vietnamese government and reunite the country under one communist regime.

Johnson continued the policy of aiding South Vietnam without committing American troops. His actions were based in part on his belief that World War II could have been avoided had the United States stood up to Nazi aggression in the 1930s. Many people believed the war in Vietnam was a civil war, but Johnson thought it was a clear case of communist aggression, an attempt by North Vietnam to take over South Vietnam by armed force. Johnson believed a withdrawal from Vietnam would only invite further communist aggression.

On August 2, in the midst of the 1964 election campaign, the White House announced that North Vietnamese gunboats had attacked the U.S. destroyer *Maddox* in the Gulf of Tonkin between North Vietnam and China. Two days later the administration announced that North Vietnamese boats had fired on the *Maddox* and another destroyer, the *C. Turner Joy.* That night President Johnson appeared on television to announce that he had ordered a bombing raid on North Vietnamese boats and their bases. It was the first American bombing of North Vietnam.

Johnson asked Congress to pass the Gulf of Tonkin Resolution, which authorized him "to take all necessary measures to repel any armed attack against the forces of the United States to prevent further aggression." Congress rarely opposes a president after he has taken military action, and the Gulf of Tonkin Resolution passed overwhelmingly. Many historians believe that Johnson created a crisis over the Gulf of Tonkin incident to involve the United States more directly in the Vietnam War. Indeed, many historians believe that the United States provoked the first attack on the *Maddox* and that the second attack may have never occurred.

In retrospect, it is virtually undeniable that the Gulf of Tonkin Resolution marked a turning point in America's role in Vietnam. At the time, most people believed the resolution only gave congressional sanction to Johnson's retaliatory bombing. But the resolution allowed the president to decide what constituted aggression and gave him a free hand to respond to it in any way he chose. The resolution began America's direct military involvement in the Vietnam War.

But this would become clear only much later. In the fall of 1964, America's attention was focused on the presidential election.

In the 6 weeks leading up to November 3, Johnson traveled 60,000 miles and made more than 200 speeches, enjoying the glow of public adulation. He shook so many hands his palms were raw. Traveling to a speech, Johnson would often stop his limousine, roll down his window, and greet people passing

I do not think that the speculation that we are losing the fight in that area, or that things have gone to pot there, are at all justified.
—LYNDON JOHNSON
an early evaluation of the Vietnam War

by. Often he would pull out a bullhorn and give a speech right on the spot, issuing his "call for national unity" and his promise that "we seek no wider war" in Vietnam.

But Johnson's support for civil rights had alienated the South. Goldwater's anti-civil-rights stand was attracting support in several southern states. Johnson was determined not to be rejected by his southern neighbors. But he also wanted to meet the racial issue head on.

On October 9, Johnson took his campaign to New Orleans. At the end of his prepared remarks to a large but not very friendly crowd in the Grand Ballroom at the Jung Hotel, Johnson decided to "talk straight" on the civil rights issue. He spoke of his sadness that so many southerners — black and white — still lived in the poverty he remembered from his childhood. The crowd grew quiet, and Johnson explained his belief that it was racial hatred that kept the South from uniting against its real enemy, the big interests.

Then Johnson leaned over the lectern to tell a story about Sam Rayburn's visit to an old southern senator many years before. Late into the night they talked about the South and its racial divisions. And then the old senator told Rayburn that he wished he felt well enough to go back to his home state and " 'make them one more Democratic speech. I just feel like I've got one in me. Poor old state, they haven't heard a real Democratic speech in thirty years,' " Johnson said. And then he raised both his arms and slashed the air as he related the old senator's words: " 'All they ever hear at election time is nigra, nigra, nigra.' "

The crowd gasped and then went silent. White southerners had heard politicians play on their racial fears for decades. Now Johnson was saying they had let themselves be manipulated. But the audience knew there was truth in what Johnson had said and that it had taken courage to say it. The applause was slow and scattered at first. But soon a few people began to stand up. And as they stood up, more people applauded. And as they began to applaud, they rose to their feet, and the applause

rose with them until it reached a roar that lasted for five minutes.

The night before the election, Lyndon and Lady Bird flew to Austin. Surrounded by the people who had helped him rise from the hill country to the Capitol, from the House to the White House, Johnson said, "It seems to me tonight that I have spent my whole life getting ready for this moment."

On November 3, 1964, Lyndon Baines Johnson won the biggest landslide victory in presidential history. Johnson had issued a "call for national unity," and more than 15 million Americans from every conceivable group — black and white, blue collar and white collar, rural and urban from the North and from the South — had answered. It was an assassin's bullet that first brought Johnson to the White House to carry out President Kennedy's program. Now the American people were sending him back to the White House to carry out his own.

On Capitol Hill, Johnson takes the oath of office from Chief Justice Earl Warren on January 21, 1965. Johnson's wide margin of victory made it possible for him to secure the passage of his Great Society legislation.

7

From the Great Society to Vietnam

Johnson believed that the size of his victory gave him a unique opportunity to implement his Great Society program. He believed very strongly that it could begin a new era of sustained prosperity, national unity, and social justice. Johnson also cared deeply about his own place in history. The election strengthened even more his confidence in his own abilities. He seemed to see everything related to his administration — from his legislative proposals down to the trappings of presidential power — as an extension of himself. To Johnson, the Great Society was "my Great Society," and each of the separate bills that made it up was "my bill." One day, while visiting an air force base, Johnson was walking toward a helicopter when a young soldier stopped him. The soldier pointed to another one a few yards away and said, "Mr. President, *that's* your helicopter." Johnson turned to the soldier and replied, "Son, they're *all* my helicopters."

We have kept our guns over the mantle . . . for a long time now. I can't ask our American soldiers out there to continue to fight with one hand tied behind their backs.
—LYNDON JOHNSON
on the Vietnam War

Johnson was reelected to the presidency during one of the most turbulent periods of American history. The 1960s were a time of conflict among nations, races, and generations, resulting in a profound reshaping of many aspects of American life.

Johnson poses with members of his cabinet in 1967. Johnson depended heavily on his advisers in deciding to increase U.S. involvement in the Vietnam war.

Yet despite the satisfaction he felt as he began his first term, Johnson believed his support was "like a western river — wide but not deep." He decided he would have to implement his program quickly, while Congress was still behind him.

Johnson may have thought the Great Society was *his* Great Society, but he decided he would have to share credit for it with Congress if he wanted to get it passed. He consulted with congressional leaders before he sent bills to Capitol Hill, even before they were written. By enlisting Congress's help in developing and enacting his agenda, Johnson made key congressmen feel that his program was their program.

Johnson developed an elaborate system of tracking legislation through Congress. At cabinet meetings he stood beside an easel holding a large chart showing where each of his bills stood in Congress. Meeting with his staff, he discussed each congressman one by one to determine how many votes he had on each bill. As a bill headed for a vote, Johnson read detailed reports about those congressmen who might be convinced to support him. The reports explained each congressman's reason for opposing a specific measure, what the congressman's priorities were, and how the congressman might be persuaded to vote Johnson's way. Several congressmen found that Johnson knew more about their political needs than their own campaign managers did.

On January 7, 1965, Johnson sent Congress a bill proposing a national health insurance system, Medicare, for people over the age of 65. The number of senior citizens had doubled since 1945, and hospital costs had increased dramatically. Medicare would help the elderly pay their medical bills. However, the proposal met with strong opposition. Insurance companies feared it would take away their business. Doctors feared it was the beginning of a system of "socialized medicine" in which the government would operate the medical industry and individual doctors would no longer be private practitioners free to set their own rates and fees. Senator Russell Long of Louisiana tried to defeat the bill by offering amendments in the Senate Finance Committee that would require a tax increase to pay for the program.

Johnson issued a combination of promises and threats to other committee members in a series of White House meetings. He promised one senator a campaign appearance in 1966 and told him that "probably there are other things we can do. You're too fine a senator to lose." Another senator related how "the president told me he understood all my problems. Then, in the nicest way — he was pouring me a soft drink — he suggested that I would face worse problems, and damn practical ones, I must say, if I didn't see the light." The committee rejected Long's amendments, and the bill passed on July 30, 1965. Johnson was quick to share credit for the new legislation. At a special ceremony, Johnson used 12 pens to sign the new law, gave them to 12 senators, and commended Long for his "effective and able work" on behalf of the bill he had tried so hard to defeat.

Only days after he sent Congress his Medicare bill, Johnson submitted a proposal for federal aid to education. Ever since Johnson had relented in his stubborn refusal to go to college, he had been a strong believer in education. He had seen in his own life how college had helped him escape the hill country. And he believed that many inequalities in American life stemmed from inequalities in education. His Elementary and Secondary Education Act pro-

With the additional congressmen that have been elected, I'll have a good chance to get my program through. Of course, for that I have to depend on you, the twenty or thirty people who are in this room.
—LYNDON JOHNSON
to his congressional
liaison officers

Johnson shakes hands with Martin Luther King, Jr., following the signing of the Civil Rights Act. Dr. King was the nation's most influential black leader and received the Nobel Peace Prize in 1964.

posed a $1.5 billion program to improve public schools, targeted particularly to aid poor students in the South and Appalachia.

President Kennedy had lost a full year trying to pass similar legislation over the opposition of Catholic groups. Johnson made sure he had their support *before* he sent his bill to Congress. Catholics had opposed the measure because the aid would go only to public schools. Johnson's bill won their support by giving both public and parochial (church-supported) schools federal funds to improve school libraries. In Congress, Johnson used all the pressure he could muster to pass the bill "without a comma changed." It passed with only minor amendments in just 87 days. After signing his education and Medicare bills, Johnson often said he wanted to be remembered as the "health and education president."

Johnson believed the United States needed a respite from the divisions created by the Civil Rights Act of 1964. He hoped to wait until 1966 before proposing new legislation on voting rights, but events quickly forced him to change his plans.

Despite significant progress on civil rights in the preceding 10 years, blacks were still denied their right to vote throughout the South. In 1965, Martin Luther King, Jr., announced a drive to register 3 million black voters. King began his effort in Selma, Alabama, where the old ways of segregation remained intact. When King led blacks to the courthouse to register to vote, Sheriff Jim Clark and his posse arrested them. On other occasions, they were clubbed and whipped.

On March 7, King led 400 blacks and whites on a 52-mile march from Selma to Montgomery, the state capital. At the Edmund Pettus Bridge over the Alabama River, Sheriff Clark and his posse were waiting. Clark ordered the marchers to turn around and head back to Selma. The marchers stopped but held their ground. The posse rode into the crowd, wielding nightsticks, bullwhips, and cattle prods. Women and children were beaten to a bloody pulp. Others ran for their lives, choking on tear gas.

Television cameras recorded the entire scene. Outrage swept the country. King declared he would lead another march to Montgomery on March 21. Many people wanted Johnson to protect the demonstrators with federal troops. But Johnson was reluctant. He believed sending federal troops over the objections of Governor George Wallace would only make Wallace a martyr to the cause of white supremacy. At a White House meeting, Johnson tried to appeal to Wallace's vanity. He told Wallace that the nation needed a governor from the Deep South who could be a symbol of racial harmony. Wallace could be that governor, if only he would "stop looking back to 1865 and start planning for 2065." Wallace was not prepared to go that far. But he said after the meeting that "if I hadn't left when I did, he'd have had me coming out for civil rights." Wallace announced that Alabama would not pay the costs of protecting the demonstrators, and he called on Johnson to send federal troops.

Johnson could now protect the demonstrators without making a hero out of Wallace. The larger issue of whether the federal government would protect the voting rights of blacks remained unresolved, however. Johnson decided to submit the Voting Rights Act to Congress immediately, instead of waiting until 1966. On March 15, he spoke before a joint session of Congress.

Not since Harry Truman had asked Congress to enact legislation to end a railroad strike in 1948 had a president gone before Congress to appeal for a specific piece of legislation. There was not an empty seat in the House chamber. A hush, broken only by the sound of clicking camera shutters, fell over the room. In a quiet, formal voice, Johnson compared the events in Selma to the opening gunshots of the American Revolution and the Civil War. He declared that the injustices suffered by American blacks struck at the very foundation of democracy. "And should we defeat every enemy, should we double our wealth and conquer the stars, and still be unequal to this issue, then we will have failed as a people and as a nation."

> *We shall seek to arouse the federal government by marching by the thousands to the places of registration. We are not asking, we are demanding the right to vote.*
> —MARTIN LUTHER KING, JR.
> Civil rights
> movement leader

Johnson's speech rose to a ringing pitch. The force of history seemed to be welling up in his voice. A southern president, a former opponent of civil rights legislation, was placing the full weight of his office behind the civil rights movement. No president, not even Lincoln, had spoken so unequivocally in favor of extending "the full blessings of American life" to black America. "The Constitution says that no person shall be kept from voting because of his race or his color. We have all sworn an oath before God to support and to defend that Constitution. We must now act in obedience to that oath. . . . This time, on this issue, there must be no delay, no hesitation, and no compromise with our purpose."

Toward the end of his speech, in the southern drawl that the nation had come to associate with bullwhips and bigotry, Johnson uttered the refrain of the civil rights movement. In a forceful tone, pausing for emphasis between each word, he said, "And . . . we . . . shall . . . overcome." Legislators on the floor of the House and citizens in the galleries above wept openly and unabashedly.

Finally, Johnson traced his strong feelings on civil rights back to his Mexican students at Welhausen Ward Elementary School in Cotulla. He knew they were poor and discriminated against. "I saw it in their eyes," he said. He had wished he could do more for them. "I never thought then, in 1928, that I would be standing here in 1965. It never occurred to me in my fondest dreams that I might have the chance to help the sons and daughters of those students and to help people like them all over the country.

"But now I do have that chance — and I'll let you in on a secret: I mean to use it. And I hope you will use it with me." Then Johnson threw a kiss to Lady Bird and his daughter Lynda in the presidential box and left the chamber.

In drafting the Civil Rights Act of 1965, Johnson instructed his aides to work closely with the Senate leadership, particularly Minority Leader Dirksen. Johnson wanted to be sure he had Republican support to forestall any attempt by southern Democrats to delay the bill. It was submitted to Congress on

March 17. The law removed local authorities from the supervision of federal elections in any county where discrimination had occurred in the 1964 election. Counties were declared discriminatory if they had used literacy or any other test to restrict voting, or if less than 50 percent of the voting-age population had cast their ballots. Under these provisions, the attorney general was authorized to supervise elections in seven southern states by sending examiners to register all qualified voters without exception.

The bill still left one issue unresolved. Poll taxes in federal elections had already been outlawed, but the new bill said nothing about poll taxes in state and local elections; such taxes still existed in many states. The White House had opposed such a ban, fearing it would be declared unconstitutional. Dirksen offered an amendment to the bill instructing the attorney general to file suits against poll taxes in Alabama, Mississippi, Texas, and Virginia. After lengthy debates and delaying tactics by southern diehards, the measure passed both houses of Congress. With Martin Luther King and other civil rights figures at his side, Johnson signed the bill on August 6 in the President's Room of the Capitol, the place where Lincoln had signed a law freeing slaves forced to fight in the Confederate army during the Civil War.

The Voting Rights Act was perhaps the most dramatic piece of legislation passed by Congress in 1965. But it was just 1 of 89 bills sponsored or supported by Johnson that Congress enacted that year, including new laws to combat air and water pollution, several antipoverty programs, $2.4 billion in federal aid to higher education, and the establishment of a new cabinet Department of Housing and Urban Development and the National Foundation for the Arts and the Humanities. In 1965 Johnson won approval for more major legislation than any president since Roosevelt's famous Hundred Days in 1933.

Despite the enormous success of Johnson's Great Society, his conduct of the Vietnam War began to attract increasingly vocal opposition. By the beginning of 1965, Johnson's military advisers decided that South Vietnam would be defeated unless the United States stepped up its involvement. On February 6, the Vietcong attacked an American airstrip in Pleiku, 240 miles northeast of Saigon, the South Vietnamese capital. Homemade hand grenades stuffed in beer cans killed eight Americans. Twelve hours after the raid Johnson ordered 49 A-4 Skyhawks and F-8 Crusaders to bomb Dong Hoi, a guerrilla stronghold 40 miles into North Vietnam. Johnson said that the bombing was in retaliation for the raid on Pleiku, but three weeks later he ordered the continuous bombing of North Vietnam.

The campaign marked a new stage in America's involvement in the war. Bombing raids after the Gulf of Tonkin incident and Pleiku had been quick reprisals for guerrilla attacks. Now the United States had embarked on a sustained campaign to "force the North Vietnamese into negotiations."

Although most Americans backed Johnson's decision, an antiwar movement began to take shape on America's college campuses. Several thousand students at the University of Michigan attended a "teach-in" on March 24. In April, teach-ins spread to other campuses. At most teach-ins, faculty and students maintained that the war in Vietnam was a mistake that ought to be brought to an end. On other campuses, however, particularly at the University of California at Berkeley, many students argued that the war had been created by a corrupt economic and political system. They believed a movement was forming that would bring an end to the war and the system that had created it.

Johnson hoped the bombing campaign would prevent the United States from having to send ground troops to Vietnam. Far from breaking the will of North Vietnam to continue the war, however, the bombing seemed only to stiffen the North's resolve. As long as support for the North remained high in South Vietnam, Hanoi (the capital of North Vietnam) could always replace its lost supplies. The bombing campaign only encouraged South Vietnam to rely more heavily on the United States. Yet Johnson feared he could not use the full power of the American military without bringing communist China or the Soviet Union into the war.

Slowly Johnson began to send ground troops to Vietnam. In March, 1,500 marines landed in Vietnam to protect an American air base near Da Nang. Then the Pentagon requested more forces to protect the troops protecting the air base. By the end of April, the United States had 50,000 men in Vietnam. And as the number of soldiers expanded, so did their mission. In April, U.S. forces were permitted to aid South Vietnamese units under siege. In June, American troops were permitted to go into combat with South Vietnamese units, and then on their own. All the while, Johnson publicly insisted that the United States was not at war.

The mounting American commitment only resulted in increased casualties and further losses of territory to the Vietcong. Many people, including Under Secretary of State George Ball, were calling for a withdrawal from Vietnam. But Johnson had no intention of ending the war. He later recalled that he was "convinced our retreat would open the path to World War III." At the end of July, Johnson decided on an immediate increase of 50,000 troops, and a further increase to 250,000 troops by November.

By 1967 antiwar protesters were demonstrating outside the White House daily. Other forms of protest for the cause of peace were sit-ins and mass draft-card burnings.

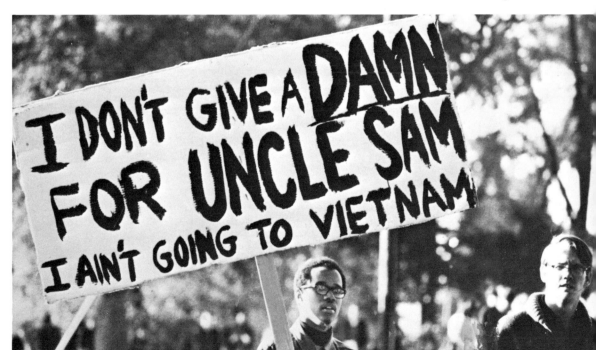

Two soldiers help a wounded friend out of a firing zone in the battle of Hue, during the Tet Offensive. The success of the North Vietnamese-Vietcong attack showed that the United States was far from victory in Vietnam and helped convince Johnson not to seek reelection.

But Johnson kept as much of his plan secret as possible. He told Congress only about the immediate increase of 50,000 troops, and he asked for an additional $1.8 billion to conduct the war. In preparing his memoirs, in several long conversations with Doris Kearns, a professor of government at Harvard University, Johnson defended his attempts to keep the scope of the war secret. He told Kearns that he "simply had no choice but to keep my foreign policy in the wings. I knew the Congress as well as I know Lady Bird, and I knew that the day it exploded into a major debate on the war, that day would be the beginning of the end of the Great Society. . . . I was determined to be a leader of war and a leader of peace. I refused to let my critics push me into choosing one or the other."

In 1966, Vietnam did become a major issue of debate in Congress, and Congress did force Johnson to choose between the Great Society and the war. Johnson increased U.S. ground troops to 383,000. More troops required more money. The administration spent $4.7 billion on the war in 1965. In 1966, the administration asked Congress for $10 billion for Vietnam, and then asked for $20 billion. Southern congressmen demanded cuts in the Great Society in return for their support on Vietnam. By the summer of 1966, Johnson turned his attention away from domestic reform and devoted almost all his energies to the war.

In November, Eric Sevareid, a respected journalist, reported that the United States had rejected a proposal for peace talks with Hanoi. The news did not square with Johnson's contention that North Vietnam had rejected U.S. proposals to begin negotiations. Many Americans became more convinced than ever that Johnson had no intention of seeking a political solution to the conflict.

The results of the 1966 congressional elections — in which the Democrats lost 47 seats in the House — seemed to be an indictment of Johnson, his party, and a war that many Americans increasingly saw as his war. Johnson had remained popular throughout 1965 despite the growth of the antiwar movement. But students had been burning draft cards for nearly a year, and his critics had become increasingly vocal and angry. Johnson deeply resented this criticism. As Senate majority leader, he had supported Eisenhower on matters of national security because he believed any other course would have been dishonorable and unpatriotic. He felt that he, too, was entitled to this support. Indeed, the louder his critics became, the more he believed they were damaging the nation.

By early 1967, Johnson believed the situation in Vietnam had improved. The South Vietnamese were capturing more enemy weapons and losing fewer of their own. Important Vietcong bases were captured. The Vietcong and North Vietnamese were suffering heavier casualties. Yet enemy forces did not decrease. There seemed to be no end to the number of North Vietnamese and Vietcong willing to die for their cause.

Johnson escalated the war again. The United States began shelling supply routes and mining rivers in North Vietnam. In April, National Security Adviser Walt W. Rostow, Secretary of Defense Robert S. McNamara, and his deputy, Cyrus Vance, recommended the bombing program be expanded.

Johnson presided over the bombing in much the same way he had presided over congressional strategy in 1965. He chose bombing targets personally, going over each of the possibilities in great detail with his aides, just as he had selected congressmen who might be persuaded to vote with him on Great Society legislation. He questioned his aides for hours about the relative importance of various targets in North Vietnam, under what circumstances they could most easily be hit, and what cost there might be in trying. Often he lay awake at night, reviewing these decisions in his mind. Clad in his pajamas, Johnson made frequent late-night visits to the White House Situation Room, seeking information on the course of the war from the Pentagon and Central Intelligence Agency (CIA) officers who gathered reports from Vietnam around the clock.

In the summer of 1967, Johnson decided to increase troop levels to 525,000 by the summer of 1968. As Johnson escalated the war, casualties

I never saw Woodrow Wilson's picture in the Red Room of the White House, never looked at it that I didn't think it might happen to me . . . I didn't want that to happen.
—LYNDON JOHNSON
on letting the presidency
destroy him

Johnson and General William Westmoreland, commander of the U.S. forces in Vietnam, arrive for Sunday church services in Fredericksburg, Texas. Westmoreland would later be accused of intentionally misleading the government about the strength of opposition forces in Vietnam.

mounted. In 1966 a total of 5,000 Americans were killed in Vietnam, and 33,000 were wounded. In 1967 there were 9,000 killed and 80,000 wounded. With the costs of the war increasing, Johnson asked for a tax increase in the summer of 1967. Congress agreed but demanded further cuts in spending on Great Society programs first. In the fall the administration said there was "light at the end of the tunnel" and that the war would soon end. General William C. Westmoreland, commander of American troops in Vietnam, said the war was going so well that the United States would soon begin to "phase down" its troop commitment and turn conduct of the war over to the South Vietnamese.

Opposition to the war continued to mount. The Pentagon had always denied North Vietnamese reports that the U.S. bombing campaign was claiming scores of civilian casualties. But American press reports at the beginning of 1967 forced the Pentagon to concede that civilians were being killed. The suffering of the North Vietnamese became a standard argument against the war. On April 15, nearly half a million people protested the war at rallies in New

York and San Francisco. Influential liberal intellectuals who had supported the war began to speak out against it. Public approval ratings of Johnson's performance as president fell from 70 percent in 1965 to just 39 percent in August 1967. Much of the anger against the war was directed at Johnson personally. Protesters demonstrated outside the White House daily, chanting, "Hey, hey, LBJ! How many kids did you kill today?" In December the antiwar movement tried to disrupt the draft with sit-ins at induction centers in New York. The sit-ins ended with 581 arrests and dozens of protesters beaten and bloodied by police.

Johnson and his advisers had expected a major attack in early 1968, but the scale of the Tet Offensive caught them completely by surprise. On January 30, during the Vietnamese Tet holidays celebrating the Lunar New Year, 84,000 North Vietnamese and Vietcong troops tried to topple the South Vietnamese government with raids on 36 provincial capitals. Food supplies and electric power were cut off in several cities, including Saigon. A suicide squad blasted a hole in the wall surrounding the United States embassy in Saigon. The United States sustained heavy casualties. The enemy lost 45,000 men in fighting over the next month, more deaths than the United States had sustained in 9 years.

The Tet Offensive failed to topple the South Vietnamese government. But the offensive also suggested that U.S. claims that the war was going well were untrue. Any force that could mount an attack as large as the Tet Offensive was clearly not on the brink of collapse.

As winter turned to spring, Johnson had to decide whether to run for reelection. Despite his declining popularity, he was expected to defeat Minnesota Senator Eugene McCarthy handily in New Hampshire's Democratic primary, held in March. But McCarthy's antiwar platform attracted far more votes than anyone expected. President Kennedy's younger brother Senator Robert Kennedy of New York, a vocal opponent of the war, entered the race four days later. Johnson believed that he could still

Antiwar protesters crowd onto Washington's Memorial Bridge during a 1967 peace march. The pressure they exerted upon the White House contributed greatly to Johnson's decision not to run for reelection in 1968.

win reelection, but he also recognized that the war had deeply divided the country. He could not conduct the war during an election campaign when his every move would be seen as a political maneuver. Johnson also had more personal considerations to take into account. His father had died of a heart attack in 1937. Johnson had suffered one in 1955, and he remembered the figure of President Woodrow Wilson, incapacitated by a stroke during his last years in the White House. Johnson did not want to end a second full term the same way.

On March 31 Johnson told the nation in a televised address that "I shall not seek, and I will not accept, the nomination of my party for another term as your president." Johnson also said that he would restrict bombing to the southern quarter of North Vietnam. On April 3, Hanoi announced its willingness to meet with American representatives for preliminary discussions on peace talks. Finally, the war seemed to be winding down.

Johnson was greatly relieved after the speech. His buoyant mood was quickly broken, however. Johnson was in his White House office on the evening after Hanoi's announcement when he was informed that Martin Luther King, Jr., had been assassinated in Memphis. He went on television that night to "ask every citizen to reject the blind violence that has

Johnson's announcement on March 31, 1968, that he would not seek reelection shocked most Americans. But his poor performance in an early primary and advice from cabinet members that he reconsider his Vietnam policy had convinced him that his candidacy would further divide the nation.

struck Dr. King, who lived by nonviolence." Despite Johnson's plea, 40 cities, including Washington, D.C., erupted in angry violence. Johnson met with black leaders the following day and decided to press for new civil rights legislation. The Civil Rights Act of 1968 made it illegal for homeowners to stipulate by race to whom their homes could be sold. The bill had been rejected in 1966 and 1967, and Johnson had resubmitted it in January 1968. The bill passed just three days after King's funeral.

Tragedy struck again on June 5. Senator Robert Kennedy was shot and killed in Los Angeles on the night of the California primary. Kennedy and Johnson had had a tense relationship dating back to Johnson's term as vice-president. Robert Kennedy had hoped his brother would choose a more liberal running mate in 1960, and Johnson had always resented Kennedy's belief that he was the true heir to his brother's legacy. Kennedy's opposition to the Vietnam war only widened the breach after 1966. Nonetheless, Johnson recalled in his memoirs that their last meeting had been friendly. "Robert Kennedy's death," he wrote, "seemed to symbolize the irrationality that was besieging our nation and the world."

There were some successes toward the end of 1968. On July 1, the United States signed a treaty on the nonproliferation of nuclear weapons with the Soviet Union and 50 other nations. In agreeing to the terms of the treaty, the signatory nations pledged not to help other countries develop nuclear weapons. On October 31, Johnson announced that the United States and North Vietnam had agreed to begin peace talks in Paris. Although the war would continue for seven more years, it appeared to be coming to an end.

A divided Democratic party nominated Vice-president Hubert Humphrey for president. The Republicans nominated Richard M. Nixon, who had served as vice-president under Eisenhower. Humphrey could never quite shake his long association with Johnson and the Vietnam War. Nixon won the November election.

> *I shall do everything in my power to move us toward peace that the new president and, I believe, every other American so deeply and urgently desires.*
> —LYNDON JOHNSON
> on negotiating a cease-fire in Vietnam

Solemn marchers accompany Martin Luther King, Jr.'s coffin as it is carried through the streets of Atlanta, Georgia. The assassination of King in April 1968 and the ongoing war in Vietnam were a bitter end to the dreams and ideals of the Great Society.

Nixon's inauguration took place on January 20, 1969, a chilly day under gray skies. In 1961, Johnson had been seated on the same platform as the incoming vice-president, with Nixon the outgoing vice-president. Now Johnson was turning his office over to Nixon. As Nixon rose to take the oath of office, he gave Johnson a blanket to warm himself against the heavy wind that whipped over the platform. Nixon asked Johnson how he felt. "This is the happiest day of my life," Johnson replied.

Johnson's presidency had begun in a flurry of reform legislation. He was a southerner who had done more for civil rights than any president in history. Yet his presidency ended with the nation divided over a seemingly endless war. He believed that his every action had been undertaken with peace as its aim, but that the country had greatly misunderstood his intentions. The war and the criticism it inspired had become painful burdens, and he was happy to turn both over to someone else.

8

Back to the Hill Country

Unlike Presidents Truman and Eisenhower, Johnson did not remain active in public life after his retirement. The peace talks in Paris proceeded slowly. President Nixon gradually began to pull troops out of Vietnam, but he expanded the U.S. bombing campaign, including secret raids on guerrilla bases in neighboring Cambodia. The Vietnam War continued to divide the nation. President Nixon also cut back on many of Johnson's Great Society programs. Yet Johnson rarely commented on national issues. Antiwar demonstrators often protested at his public appearances, so he kept them to a minimum. He believed that the nation had neither appreciated nor understood him, and that there was no longer much he could do to change this.

Still, Johnson kept a close watch on public affairs. Each Friday a courier arrived from Washington carrying a briefcase full of intelligence reports on the war and other national security matters. President Nixon frequently called Johnson for his advice. CIA director Richard Helms, and General Westmoreland, now army chief of staff, occasionally came to the LBJ Ranch to brief Johnson personally.

Along this stream and under these trees he loved he will now rest. He first saw light here. He last felt life here. May he now find peace here.
—JOHN CONNALLY governor of Texas, at Johnson's Texas hill country burial

A proud grandfather, Johnson holds his week-old grandson Patrick Lyndon Nugent on his knee. Retirement afforded him more time to spend with his family.

Johnson at the dedication of the LBJ Park in 1971. Concerned about his historical reputation, Johnson established the Johnson Presidential Library on the campus of the University of Texas in Austin.

As a former president, Johnson received a government grant to run an office he kept in Austin that handled the hundreds of letters he received each day. A military helicopter was available to him at all times. He was also assigned a Secret Service detail. The Secret Service men laid out his clothes in the morning, gave him a rubdown at night, and followed him everywhere he went. Several former aides helped Johnson prepare his memoirs, and they made themselves available to him at all hours for work and companionship.

Johnson found the adjustment to private life very difficult at first. For 20 years there had not been enough hours in the day to see all the people who sought his attention, to address all the issues that awaited his decision. So he applied his remarkable energy and attention to detail to the affairs of his ranch. He made himself chief executive of the LBJ Ranch. He presided over daily meetings with his staff, questioning them closely on their work the same way he had questioned his White House aides. He spent hours each day driving around the ranch, checking up on his men. He had them write daily reports, which he read each night the same way he had read intelligence reports before he went to bed in the White House.

Eventually, however, Johnson settled down in his retirement. The presidency had not given him much time for his family, and he had some catching up to do. His relationship with Lady Bird was very close and affectionate. He liked to tease her, particularly about her management of their financial affairs. Aides noticed that they often held hands when they were together and greeted each other affectionately after short separations.

He also enjoyed spending time with his daughters Lynda and Luci. They were married now and had given him two grandchildren. He seemed to display remarkable patience with them. He entertained them for hours at a time, taking an almost childlike pleasure in their games long after most adults would have turned to something else. He also spent a lot of time with friends, watching movies, or enjoying a quiet dinner.

Johnson set himself three tasks for his last years in Texas. He wanted to oversee the plans for the establishment of the Lyndon B. Johnson School of Public Affairs and the Lyndon B. Johnson Presidential Library, both at the University of Texas in Austin. The library was built in appropriately grand Johnson style. It was eight stories of white traver-

Lines of people wait outside the Johnson Library to pay their last respects to the former president. A few days later, he was taken to Washington for state services.

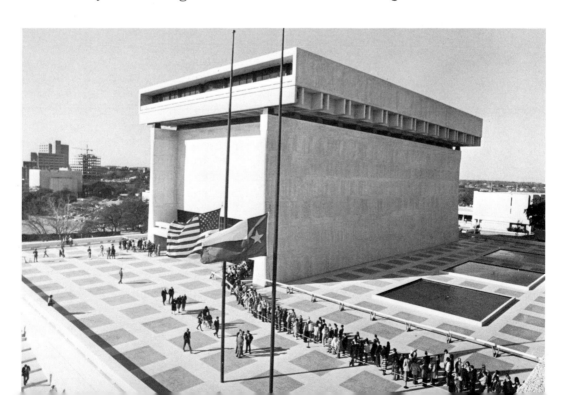

tine marble with a helicopter pad on the roof. It housed 31 million papers, larger than the entire manuscript collection of the Library of Congress. Johnson's critics called it "Lyndon's Mausoleum," but Johnson said he wanted historians to be able to document his entire presidency. "I want it all there with the bark off, what I did right and what I did wrong," he said. Johnson kept a close watch on attendance figures at the library, believing they were an indication of history's final verdict on his presidency.

Johnson found writing his memoirs very difficult. He had hoped to complete three volumes covering his entire life from the hill country to the White House. But he completed only the one describing his presidency, *The Vantage Point: Perspectives of the Presidency*. He found the act of writing too passive for his active nature. So he spent long hours talking to his aides, describing important events, and reading from stacks of documents that had influenced his decisions.

Johnson's presidential memoir, *The Vantage Point: Perspectives of the Presidency*, was published in 1971. The former president found writing a very difficult task.

Johnson and Lady Bird in 1973. Johnson's presidency remains controversial. Some criticize him as the man responsible for increased U.S. involvement in the Vietnam War, while others praise him for his support of the civil rights movement and his innovative social-welfare programs.

He spent a great deal of time talking to one aide in particular: Doris Kearns, a Harvard political scientist. She had been a White House fellow, one of a group of promising young scholars who get practical experience by working in government. Kearns worked in the Labor Department and then came over to the White House during the last few months of 1968. Johnson believed liberal intellectuals, many of them from Harvard, had never given him a fair hearing and had contributed to his loss of public support. Although Kearns had criticized the Vietnam War in an article she wrote before becoming a White House fellow, she also came from a modest background, like Johnson. They had a good rapport. He hoped that by explaining his presidency to Kearns he might reach the larger intellectual community of which she was a part. After Johnson left the White House, Kearns commuted between Harvard and Austin. She and Johnson spent hours together talking about his life and his presidency. In 1976 she wrote her own book, analyzing Johnson's character and its impact on his conduct in the Senate and the White House. She did not see everything Johnson's way. But her book is an insightful and dispassionate description of Johnson and his public life.

Johnson seemed to age dramatically in his retirement. His hair turned white, and the sharp creases in his face deepened. He suffered from pains in his stomach and chest. His doctors told him he was in good health, but Johnson believed he was dying. "I've got an instinct," he told Kearns. Johnson had a heart attack on March 2, 1970. He recovered at Brooke General Hospital, an army facility in San Antonio. Two years later he suffered another heart attack, at the home of his daughter Lynda and her husband, Charles Robb, in Farmington, Virginia. This heart attack was more serious than the one in 1970, and Johnson returned to the LBJ Ranch for a long recuperation.

Richard Nixon was inaugurated for a second term in January 1973. On January 21, Nixon announced that a cease-fire had been reached with North Vietnam. The long war that brought down Johnson's presidency was finally coming to an end. Nixon also unveiled a plan to dismantle the Great Society. The greatest achievement of the Johnson presidency seemed to be coming to an end as well. The following day, Johnson suffered a fatal heart attack while taking an afternoon nap.

Johnson's successor in the White House, Richard Nixon, announced a cease-fire in the Vietnam War on January 21, 1973. Johnson suffered a fatal heart attack the next day.

Nixon never fully succeeded in dismantling the Great Society, and much of it still survives today. Johnson's presidency is still very controversial. But ironically, the debate is completely the reverse of the one that raged while he was still in office. Then, observers lamented his persistence in a futile war at the expense of his achievements on behalf of the poor and oppressed. And though many people still blame Johnson for Vietnam, now the verdict seems to be that it was not the war but the Great Society, that went too far.

Historians will no doubt debate Johnson's presidency for years to come. Many will remember him as a reformer and the greatest civil rights president the nation ever had. Many will remember him as a war chief. Still others will recall him as a tragic combination of the two. Such is the mixed blessing of his legacy.

Johnson's body is laid to rest beneath the gnarled oak trees at the family cemetery on the LBJ Ranch. He was buried beside his mother and father.

Further Reading

Bell, John L. *The Johnson Treatment: How Lyndon B. Johnson Took Over the Presidency and Made It His Own.* New York: Harper & Row, 1965.

Caro, Robert A. *The Years of Lyndon Johnson: The Path to Power.* New York: Knopf, 1982.

Evans, Rowland, and Robert Novak. *Lyndon B. Johnson: The Exercise of Power.* New York: New American Library, 1966.

Goldman, Eric F. *The Tragedy of Lyndon Johnson.* New York: Knopf, 1969.

Johnson, Lyndon B. *The Vantage Point: Perspectives of the Presidency, 1963–1969.* New York: Holt, Rinehart and Winston, 1971.

Kearns, Doris. *Lyndon Johnson and the American Dream.* New York: Harper & Row, 1976.

Miller, Merle. *Lyndon: An Oral Biography.* New York: Putnam, 1980.

Powers, Thomas. *Vietnam: The War at Home.* New York: Grossman, 1973.

Chronology

Aug. 27, 1908	Lyndon Baines Johnson born in Stonewall, Texas
1937–1948	Represents Texas's 10th District in House of Representatives
Sept. 1948	Elected to the U.S. Senate
1951–1952	Serves as Democratic party whip in the Senate
1953–1955	Serves as Senate minority leader
1955–1960	Presides over the Senate as majority leader
July 1960	Loses Democratic nomination for president to John F. Kennedy; accepts offer to be Kennedy's running mate
1961–1963	Serves as vice-president of the United States
Nov. 22, 1963	Kennedy assassinated in Dallas; Johnson takes oath as 36th U.S. president
Feb. 26, 1964	Johnson signs the Tax Reduction Act
July 2, 1964	Signs the Civil Rights Act; bans segregation and discrimination by federally funded institutions
Aug. 4, 1964	Orders retaliatory bombing of North Vietnam for attacks on U.S. vessels in Gulf of Tonkin
Nov. 3, 1964	Wins reelection in a landslide victory over Barry Goldwater
Feb. 1965	Orders sustained bombing campaign against North Vietnam
March 1965	Sends 1,500 marines to Vietnam to protect air base near Da Nang
April 1965	Commits 50,000 troops to Vietnam
April 11, 1965	Signs the Elementary and Secondary Education Act
July 30, 1965	Signs law creating Medicare
Aug. 6, 1965	Signs Civil Rights Act; protects minority voting rights
1966	Increases troops in Vietnam to 383,000 and asks Congress for $20 billion for war effort
April 15, 1967	Five hundred thousand Americans demonstrate in San Francisco against the Vietnam War
1967	Johnson increases U.S. troops in Vietnam to 523,000
Jan. 30, 1968	North Vietnamese and Vietcong troops attack South Vietnam
March 31, 1968	Johnson announces he will not run for reelection
April 3, 1968	North Vietnam announces willingness to discuss peace talks
April 4, 1968	Martin Luther King, Jr., assassinated
April 10, 1968	Civil Rights Act passes; bans discrimination in housing
June 5, 1968	Robert Kennedy assassinated
Jan. 20, 1969	Johnson leaves office; Richard M. Nixon inaugurated as 37th U.S. president
May 22, 1971	Johnson dedicates his library at the University of Texas in Austin
Jan. 21, 1973	Cease-fire with North Vietnam announced
Jan. 22, 1973	Lyndon Baines Johnson dies of a heart attack on his Texas ranch

Index

Tony Kaye is a free-lance writer living in New York. His work has appeared in *The New Republic, The Nation,* and *Nuclear Times.* Since graduating from Columbia University in 1984, he has served as research director of the Democracy Project and as senior staff associate at the New York University Center for War, Peace, and the News Media.

Arthur M. Schlesinger, jr., taught history at Harvard for many years and is currently Albert Schweitzer Professor of the Humanities at City University of New York. He is the author of numerous highly praised works in American history and has twice been awarded the Pulitzer Prize. He served in the White House as special assistant to Presidents Kennedy and Johnson.

PICTURE CREDITS

AP/Wide World Photos: pp. 27, 29, 32, 36, 38, 42, 53, 56, 59, 64, 104; Washington, D.C. Public Library: pp. 20, 28, 46, 47, 91, 95; Freelance Photographers Guild, Inc.: pp. 2, 12, 15; Library of Congress: p. 44; Lyndon Baines Johnson Library: pp. 18, 68; National Archives: p. 71; Texas State Library: p. 102; The Bettmann Archive: pp. 34, 62, 82; UPI/Bettmann Newsphotos: pp. 14, 16, 19, 24, 25, 30, 35, 39, 48, 50, 51, 54, 58, 63, 66, 67, 75–78, 81, 84, 86, 92, 94, 96, 98–100, 103, 105–107